D0065023

Modern European Culture and Consciousness, 1870–1980

SUNY Series in Interdisciplinary Perspectives in Social History
Harvey J. Graff, Editor

Modern European Culture and Consciousness, 1870–1980

Paul Monaco

State University of New York Press • *Albany*

For PATRICIA REINHARDT MONACO
whose spirit, intelligence, poetic voice, and commitment to the life
of the mind have enriched my own life so much in so many ways

Published by State Univesity of New York Press, Albany

©1983 State University of New York

For information, address State University of New York Press, State University Plaza,
Albany, N.Y., 12246

Library of Congress Cataloging in Publication Data

Monaco, Paul.
  Modern European culture and consciousness, 1870–1970.

  (SUNY series on interdisciplinary perspectives in social history)
  Bibliography: p. 129
  1. Europe—Civilization—19th century. 2. Europe—Civilization—20th century. I.
Title. II. Series.
CB204.M66 1983   940.5   82-10487
ISBN 0-87395-702-4
ISBN 0-87395-703-2 (pbk.)

Contents

With Thanks and Appreciation

To Rudolph Binion, Leff Professor of History at Brandeis University. His careful working through of my manuscript, and his pointed comments on it, have improved it greatly.

To Elizabeth G. Strebel of SUNY-Binghamton. I have long admired her research on film and society in Europe, and I value the criticisms of my manuscript which she has shared with me.

To Robert Plant Armstrong, my colleague in Dallas. His books have changed my way of thinking about art. His friendship has helped me often.

To several of my students in graduate seminars on European thought and culture who have inspired me more than they will likely ever know—Alan Baron; Gisela DeMarco; Tim Jernigan; James Kirk; Dennis Madden; Julien Riepe; Sheryl St. Germain; Marie Vaulon.

To Harvey J. Graff, an historian and a colleague of the first rank. It was he who urged me to undertake the writing of this book, and he who encouraged me by his repeated expressions of confidence in me.

Paul Monaco
Fall, 1982

Prologue

To MANY NORTH AMERICANS who might pause to think about it, Europe is like an aging dowager with a grand past but little future. She has seen much and lived through many experiences, some of them ennobling and inspiring. In the twentieth century, however, she has witnessed several of the bleakest and most troubling episodes known to humankind. Europe is a place of history, relics, and visible charm, frequently perceived as a kind of living museum to a dying Western culture. Recently a faculty colleague expressed to me his bewilderment about my teaching a course on Europe since 1945. Was it not the case, he thought, that Europe was moribund, its eclipse nearly complete, and its significance spent? Such notions are widely held.

Beyond this common perception lies a complex reality. During the 1970s per capita income in several Western European nations surpassed that of the United States. Ideologically, Western Europeans are prolific, and expressions of their political thinking are provocative and compelling, both on the Left and on the Right. In the spheres of formal and academic thought and the sciences and technology, Western Europeans compete, and well, with the Soviets, the North Americans, and the Japanese.

Many a Western European decries and condemns the undermining by North American influences of traditional elements of European culture since 1945. There is ample documentation of this phenomenon, often called pejoratively the Coca-Colonization of Western Europe. Cultural change in Europe since 1945, however, is no simple matter, and cannot easily be reduced to fit this colorful description. If Western Europe has been extensively Americanized in the last thirty-five years, at the same time the United States has been to a certain degree Europeanized. The cultural critic George Steiner has even suggested that it is the United States rather than Europe that is becoming the museum culture of the Western world.

Since its inception, public television in the United States has been dependent on program imports from Great Britain. It was the Beatles from Liverpool who assured the assimilation of rock music into the mainstream of American white middle-class culture in the 1960s. The Continental European discovery of the allure of blue jeans was the evident precondition for their transformation from work clothes into the unisex item of sportswear par excellence in the United States during the 1970s. During the 1960s and 1970s motion pictures produced in Italy, or in France, or in the German Federal Republic, were widely shown in the United States, especially in the larger urban areas. The artistic and ideological elements of the Western European cinema became the common model for many in the younger generation of film-makers in the United States. European directors have brought a different kind of vision to the screen, and in doing so they have altered the structure of that venerable institution of American culture, the Hollywood "system." In many fields of the natural sciences, in numerous academic disciplines, in medicine, and in technology, the number of persons of European birth or training at work in the United States is great. Frequently they, and their thinking, dominate entire areas of inquiry. If not actually resident in the United States, Western Europeans may still set the course in methodology and theory for many intellectual enterprises among North Americans. The pervasive influence of structuralism, originating primarily in France, is a good example of this.

Given all this, it might be apt to speak of a common Euro-American culture that has developed since 1945. Additionally, it may be that this Euro-American culture is becoming increasingly the core of what may yet emerge as a common global culture. This culture is held together by the electronic communications media and by air transportation. Its creativity is characterized by a panorama of permutations and elaborations that it has spawned and that may spring at any time from any corner of it. This is a crosscurrent, and indeed a notable one, that contradicts much received wisdom about contemporary Western culture. Recognition of it cuts against the notion of Western culture as being necessarily in a downward spiral of disarray and disintegration. Viewed from almost any perspective, it calls into question the widespread notion that Western Europe and its civilization are in eclipse.

Today, more than ever before, ideas which originated (and which continue to originate and to be elaborated) in the heartland of industrialized Western Europe—France, the British Isles, Germany-Austria, and Italy—prevail everywhere in the world. All the notions that are fundamental to contemporary life may be traced to Western European origins. These include democratization, secularization, progress through science and technology, the organizing of economic activity into industrial systems, inspired change through reform or revolution, individual liberty, social justice, national sovereignty, national citizenship, and human rights.

Any recognition of this points to an irony. As Western Europe's global fortunes have declined in terms of overt diplomatic, political, economic, or colonial influences upon other parts of the world, her intellectual and cultural influence has increased. Moreover, Western Europe appears to stand closer to the interests, concerns, and perceptions of the Third World today than do either the United States or the Soviet Union. This is so, in part, by default, given the political, diplomatic, and cultural heavy-handedness of both the superpowers. The United States and the Soviet Union have each demonstrated an awkward inability to carry on the main ideological and cultural traditions that originated in Western Europe.

Morally and spiritually the Second World War proved to be both troubling and humbling for Western Europe. By contrast, the war provided to both the United States and the Soviet Union presumptive grounds for arrogance and self-righteousness. Specifically, after 1945 the United States took up the global promotion of the "American Way of Life." The Soviet Union, with utter disregard for its own record of governmental terror and murder, asserted its solidarity with "people's movements" everywhere. Hence the posture of the United States degenerated quickly into a comparatively empty promoting of modernization as rampant consumerism, and of political progress as simple anti-Communism. This has produced two main consequences: (1) a sorry record of American inconsistency in the support of democratization and human rights; (2) the appearance, accepted widely, that the United States is simply carrying on the exploitative policies of late-nineteenth-century imperialism. The Soviet Union, in turn, pursues a global policy of seeking territorial aggrandizment under the disguise of aiding "progressive" political forces. Soviet society itself provides only a model of a technocratic party dictatorship in which crude collectivization and police terror have erased any semblance of genuine socialism.

During the two decades after the Second World War, the European powers lost their overseas empire. British and French interests, in particular, eroded quickly. In differing ways, the United States and the Soviet Union have both based their foreign policies in the postwar era on the attempt to establish their own spheres of influence in places where colonialism as such was ending. The result is a shifting relationship of Western Europe toward what has come to be called the "Third World." Whereas the superpowers, because of their opposing interests, are not in a position to do so, Western Europe can better play "honest broker" with regard to the emerging and developing nations of the world. At the heart of this Western European position is the highly salutary reorientation of thought and culture that was precipitated by the Second World War. Pushed to the edge of the abyss by the excesses of ideology and of nihilism, since 1945 Western Europe has swiftly gained back the humanizing and humane aspects of modern thought and culture. In the tempering of aggressive nationalism—which was itself an important dynamic in imperialist expansionism—Western Europe since 1945 has attained a potential new role in the world.

By certain standards, the United States, or Japan, or the Soviet Union, may be considered more successful contemporary societies than any in Europe. By the standards of thorough and thoughtful exploration of what confronts us all as humans in the modern world, however, they are not. That confrontation goes beyond the maintaining and advancing of livable cities, social and political justice, economic opportunity or public welfare, protection of the environment, population planning, and so on. In Western European thought and ideology these issues are addressed. In Western European works of the imagination, however, the greater issues of consciousness of the human predicament in the modern age are most skillfully explored. These include the nature of authentic freedom and liberation, questions of responsibility and identity in a depersonalized society, and choices such as personal commitment as opposed to escapism.

Consciousness is not determined simply by poltical realities, social circumstances, and material conditions (such as the production and distribution of goods). Consciousness is invested with a dynamic of its own, that I have decided to approach in this book through three of its divisions: individual consciousness, revolutionary consciousness, and reactionary consciousness.

Chapter One
Culture and the Past

Defining terms and concepts, and selecting and arranging materials, are fundamental to the writing of any kind of history. Behind each choice is the matter of justification: why those concepts, that material, that arrangement? In the writing of what is called "cultural history," such concerns are more problematic, perhaps, than in the undertakings of political, diplomatic, or social history.

In this essay an initial assumption is that beyond denoting a geographical place, or referring to what was once a relatively unified political entity, the term "European" itself is a cultural designation. To say so is neither alarming nor original; nonetheless, it does bear saying. Shared values, perceptions, and ideas constitute the historic European community. That community is the core of what is commonly called Western civilization. It is also the authentic center of all the varieties of European historical experience, containing within itself the differences and antagonisms among the European peoples.

The expression through works of the imagination of those shared ideas, values, and perceptions in the direction of consciousness is our topic. The ways in which these have been brought to expression have differed from place to place, from group to group, and over time. Cultural history, as commonly understood, has much to do with reconstructing these shifts, studying the influences that gave rise to them, and analyzing the crosscurrents generated by them. One particular ethnic or linguistic group among the Europeans may be cited as having dominated a particular cultural movement or a specific form of expression. This fact is commonplace in our knowledge of the Western world's cultural past. Combined with other factors, recognition of this has led to a situation in which specific national cultural traditions in Europe are often regarded as definitive. The propagation of the concept of national cultural heritage has been influenced not only by presumably objective attempts to read the historical record, but also by ideology: namely, the rise of modern nationalism since the late eighteenth century. This sort of tunnel vision on national cultural histories is not without value. Such an approach, however, is not unproblematic. For there is ample evidence of European cultural unity, over and above national distinctions, even in the modern and contemporary age.

Normally, in scholarly enterprises, as well as in everyday thinking, the differences between the ethnic or linguistic groups in Europe are emphasized. This is really an overemphasis. By contrast, part of the agenda here is to treat Western Europe holistically. This is an uphill struggle, especially when the last one hundred years are being considered—a period which, to many observers, appears to bear witness time and again to differences rather than to unity. While the matter is complex, only a few comments directed to it must suffice here.

Among the various peoples of Western Europe differences in language, religion, traditions, and institutions appear to be obvious. In fact, these differences are the subject of much of the work of historians of Europe. Differences in cuisine, personal habits, and physical apperance among the European peoples also draw attention. Attempts to reach conclusions from rather vague and unsystematic data regarding these distinctions characterize much of the popular mentality regarding national traits.

The real significance of national distinctions that are relatively concrete and verifiable, such as linguistic differences, is a matter of controversy. There is no disputing that in Western Europe a number of different languages are spoken. But just what does this mean? Can this fact undermine or seriously compromise the holistic approach to Western European culture? Since the Second World War it has become common in Western Europe for almost all youngsters who attend school to learn something of a second language. Nearly anywhere in Western Europe, when an adolescent continues academic education beyond the age of fourteen, the learning of a second language is mandatory, and the pedagogy in force is sophisticated and demanding. Historically, educated Europeans have known at least one second language. In the latter part of this century, the number of people being educated has increased enormously, and those who have at least some knowledge of a second language are numerous. Language may, in certain instances, determine profound cultural differences, but there are only two major language groups in Western Europe: Germanic and Romance.

Since the sixteenth century, most of Europe has been divided religiously between Catholicism and Protestantism, with many orders and sects. While often competing, and even belligerent toward one another, they share a common professed Christianity. Furthermore, the ecumenical movement begun at Vatican II in 1962 erased the theological basis for most of the historic divisions between Catholics and Protestants.

Political and institutional differences between the European peoples appear to be many, but on closer inspection almost all are variations on a few models. And the differences between models have tended to disappear. As for political structures, in the mid-eighteenth century only Great Britain, the Netherlands, and Switzerland were not absolute monarchies. By 1975 all the Western European states had become representative democracies. Monarchies survive, with a primarily ceremonial function, in Great Britain, Spain, Belgium, the Netherlands, and Scandinavia; they have disappeared in Austria, Italy, France and Germany.

In popular thinking in the Western world, there is a hidden assumption that the evolution of different ethnic and linguistic groups into sovereign national political entities reflects a propensity of human nature. However, the historical development of Europe along these lines was actually a result of specific circumstances. The breakdown of the political, cultural, and linguistic unity of Europe—with Latin as the common language of serious discourse—began with the conflict between secular and religious authorities, and was finalized by the Protestant Reformation in the sixteenth century. That this breakdown occurred is not in doubt. That it had to occur is neither a necessary consequence of human nature nor a function of any dynamic inherent in European civilization. Institutions existed through the Middle Ages— such as feudalism, serfdom, the church—which provided a basis for European development in the direction of unity.

Nonetheless, Europe broke up and coalesced nationally. This was the common and prevailing course of its history from the late Middle Ages to 1945. In central and eastern Europe empires composed of various ethnic and linguistic groups survived either under the dynasties of the Habsburgs or of the Russian tsars into the twentieth century. In Western Europe, attempts at unity prior to 1945 consisted of ambitious military attempts to assert the hegemony of French rule (i.e., Napoleon's campaigns, 1800–1815) or of German rule (i.e., Hitler's war, 1939–1945) upon others. The movement that began early in the 1950s toward Western European unity on a parliamentary basis marks the first genuine attempt at peaceful cooperation among the various ethnic or linguistic groups of Europe since the Middle Ages. On either economic or moral grounds, Western Europeans have widely recognized since 1945 the need to evolve beyond nationalism toward community, unity, and integration. This new recognition constitutes a major redirecting of the mainstream of historical experience since the Renaissance.

THE MODERN WORLD

Just what counts as the beginning of the modern world is a problem. The origins of the politics and economics, societies and life-styles, arts and sciences, ideas and ideologies that are agreed upon as "modern" may be traced back to the Renaissance, to the Reformation, to the scientific revolution at the end of the seventeenth century, to the start of industrialization in the eighteenth century, or to the French Revolution begun in 1789 and the Napoleonic wars, which lasted a decade and a half into the nineteenth century.

To sort out these points of departure, the Renaissance, the Reformation, and the culmination of the scientific revolution were all precipitating conditions for the modern age. They produced the intellectual and cultural shifts that underlie later developments. The precipitating factors for modern society and consciousness were as follows: (1) the emergence of rudimentary capitalism and industrialism in England in the early eighteenth century; (2) the Enlightenment and the French Revolution in the second half of the eighteenth century; (3) the appearance, at the very end of the eighteenth century, of romanticism, which is characterized by subjectivism, individualism, imagination and sensibility, as opposed to classicism and rationalism.

"Modern" experience consists extensively of continuing efforts to mediate effectively between these three main factors. Those efforts were in evidence throughout the nineteenth century, but after 1870 they took on new significance.

The political changes alone in the single year 1870–1871 were telling: (1) the unification of Germany under Prussian aegis was completed; (2) the political unification of Italy, sealed by stripping the pope of a claim to sovereignty over Rome and surrounding lands, was completed; (3) the start of the first enduring republic in a major European state, France, occurred. These three events were interrelated, and each had its own complicated prehistory. All three marked the culmination of political and ideological processes that had begun in the first half of the nineteenth century (German and Italian unification), or even earlier, with the proclamation in 1792 of the first republic in France.

The decade of the 1870s marked the beginning of an era of new and accelerated development in industry and marketing and, concurrently, of the imperialist scramble, a competition among the European nations to establish colonial management in various parts of Africa, Asia, and the Middle East. This "new" imperialism—aimed at political and economic control of distant lands rather than conquest of them for settlement—was closely linked to the "Second Industrial Revolution." Dramatic changes in corporate structure and finance capital and the advent of many new technologies marked the era. Between 1870 and 1900 the basis of material existence was entirely altered. Among the new technologies and inventions were electrification, chemicals and petrochemicals, bakelite (the forerunner of plastic), the telephone, wireless telegraphy, refrigeration, advanced production of steel, the motion picture, and the internal combustion engine.

Not all these new inventions and products were fully exploited in the era before the outbreak of the First World War. Nonetheless, they provided the basis for a consumer-oriented society, as well as the need for capital-intensive financing of industrial undertakings and access to overseas sources of raw materials. Only after 1870 was there a framework within which the twentieth century consumer societies, characterized by extensive individual discretionary consumption of goods and services, could evolve. A notable precondition for this evolution was a shift within the labor force toward more skilled and better paying jobs.

In many instances, the new inventions altered human communication, transportation, and consciousness. Electrification permitted development of streetcars and of cheaper, cleaner, long-distance trains. It was also the basis for the later technologies that permit transmission of images, sounds, or information in motion: radio, motion pictures, television, and computers. The greatest impact in communications before 1914, however, was the advent of high-speed printing for the mass-market daily press.

In roughly the same period, between 1870 and 1914, a number of intellectual currents simultaneously flourished and came under challenge. In the last quarter of the nineteenth century rationalism was still in the ascendent, with its confidence that human thought, behavior, and society could be understood and controlled as functions of enlightened self-interest. Positivism spread; sociology was founded; experimental psychology was institutionalized. The triumphs of research and inquiry in the natural sciences furthered this cause. In some instances, such as with the social implications derived from Darwin's ideas in the *Origin of Species* (1859), developments in natural science were carried over to the understanding of society—whether or not this was appropriate. Other connecting links were more obscure.

The process begun by enlightened thinkers in the early 1700s, by which the natural sciences were pushed into the forefront of Western thought and became the most admired of showpieces of human reason, seemed complete.

As with many phenomena of the last hundred years, however, a reversal followed quickly. What is interesting about this is not simply that it reflects a dialectical process—the rise of opposition to something established before—but that the swiftness of the occurrence in this instance reflects the tempo, mood, and character that set the twentieth century apart from all prior epochs. Since the early years of this century, the natural sciences have come to be regarded in a number of quarters as recondite, overspecialized, and remote from human concerns.

The nineteenth-century division between pure science, on the one hand, and the technology that lives off science, on the other, has evaporated. For many, this ever-closer linking of science and technology has drawn the natural sciences further into hostile territory. That hostile territory is an ideological as well as an intellectual terrain. It is characterized by several concerns: 1) science exploited industrially; 2) science used to intervene in human reproduction or experiments in genetic engineering; 3) corporate and governmental management of scientific technology for profit and war; 4) the advent of machinery and technologies that challenge humankind by thinking as well as, and usually much more quickly than, men and women do about some kinds of problems or by being able to retrieve certain sorts of information. The notion advanced by the British scientist and novelist C. P. Snow at the end of the 1950s of Western culture's division into two hostile camps, one scientific and the other literary or humanistic, appears to many observers to be on target. Such a perception is historically telling; had it been advanced barely sixty years earlier it would have seemed highly inaccurate and implausible.

Another reversal that has occurred in roughly the same time span is the decline of faith in rationalism. This decline has many aspects.

One of the more interesting of these is that a particular line of rationalistic scientific inquiry contributed to underwriting and popularizing a retreat from rationalism. In the 1860s scientific inquiry into the nature of the unconscious was pioneered by experimental psychologists and physiologists. Since Sigmund Freud, this has become an arena in which evidence of the powerful wellsprings of human irrationality is increasingly abundant. Freud's forerunners were concerned with studying the general conditions that evoke human awareness. Freud shifted the emphasis to a concern for the pathological loss of awareness (in neurosis or through repression), pursuing this concern from a rationalistic and scientific basis. As he proceeded, he came to revise his theory of motivation, postulate a death instinct, and entertain doubts about curing neuroses. His intellectual odyssey in search of understanding the wellsprings of human thought, action, and behavior washed ashore in the conclusion that although reason is essential to understanding, it does not control thought and behavior. Thus does the legacy of psychoanalysis eventually become a source of endorsement for antirationalist views and for an abiding pessimism.

One of the distinguishing aspects of most twentieth-century societies in the Western world is their pluralism. This is a function, in part, of the variety of freedoms present—at least on and off—in many of them. It is also a function of the history of thought and culture: ideas, allegiances, and perspectives which many a so-called *modern* of any epoch believes are dead continue to survive. This atavism is an authentic factor and a troublesome one, especially in the modern age. Those who style themselves progressives, liberals, or radicals, or men and women who simply believe in human reason and progress, can rarely abide this atavism; nor do they seem equipped, either intellectually or emotionally, to comprehend the phenomenon. In the twentieth century the agglomeration of population, the proliferation of communications systems and networks, and the democratization of many aspects of intellectual, cultural, and educational life render the survivals of older ideas all the more important. It is much the same with social relations and social institutions. Even a convinced Marxist takes it as axiomatic that the emergence of new ones does not totally exclude, but in fact incorporates, elements and traces of the old.

The Christian heritage, for example, both in thought and in feeling, remains residual in the Western world even in the face of spreading secularization, the decline in church membership (especially in northern Europe and in Great Britain), and evidence of widespread hostility or indifference to both formal religious institutions and to almost any brand of theodicy. Similarly, the secular humanist tradition, which goes back to the Renaissance, remains alive in many quarters, surviving despite both its enemies and those who presumably are its friends. The formalized rationalist creed, initially articulated by René Descartes (1596–1650) and later popularized in France in the mid-eighteenth century, maintains its vitality, here and there, on and off. The challenges to this rationalism, the record of its shortcomings in dealing with issues of public policy and social regulation, its failure to account fully for human knowing and understanding—none of these has been sufficient, either singly or in combination, to negate its fundamental premises. The central notion of eighteenth-century rationalism was that of "Political Man." This view endorsed and propagated the idea that humanity's vocation on earth was neither to seek communion with God in preparation for the afterlife nor to give itself over to introspection. Rather, human beings should develop and exercise political rights, through which both the individual and society will attain greatest fulfillment. The pursuit of liberty and personal happiness through the apparatus of politics is endorsed under the claim that free individual aspiration, combined with an awareness of issues of human and social consequence, offers the clearest path to human perfectibility.

Economic thought in the second half of the eighteenth century—for example, the physiocrats in France and Adam Smith in England—was concerned primarily with the wealth of the nation. The definition of economics as central to experience and consciousness occurred in the nineteenth century. The notion of "Economic Man" arose, to large extent, as a reaction to the inadequacy of a strictly political definition of liberty, equality, and opportunity. This particular gap was recognized before the end of the eighteenth century, in mid-phase of the French Revolution proper, by Gracchus Babeuf and his followers. By mid-nineteenth century Karl Marx had converted this frustration into a worldview, according to which the economic basis of a society determines its political, social, and cultural institutions, as well as the modes of human consciousness within it. Subsequent to Marx's "discovery" in the mid-nineteenth century, this notion, or a derivation of it, has become an ever-present centerpiece on the intellectual banquet table of the modern Western world. (It has also been resisted and debunked in the twentieth century, though more notably so in North America than in Western Europe.)

Dovetailing with these established and persisting currents is the notion, which has become apparent only in the twentieth century, of "Psychological Man." This perspective on humanity challenges the notion of humans controlling the social environment through a simple combination of law and personal motivation, both rationally derived. It also raises the question whether the triumph of civilization may in fact be harmful to the individual, and takes the sphere of economics to be only one, and perhaps a marginal, aspect of the human condition. The psychological perspective reinforces various perceptions of a fundamental hostility between the social world and the individual. Hence, the consciousness attained by accommodating oneself to "social reality" is gained at a high price indeed. Happiness and fulfillment in this context are seen as contingent upon bringing the surface, conscious level of personality into accord with the deeper, latent sources of who and what we are. This central intention is perhaps best expressed in Carl Gustav Jung's term "individuation." This process requires an effort to align ego consciousness (i.e., personality) with the bifurcated unconscious, which is divided between an individual component and a collective one. This aligning may have little or nothing to do with the realms of experience referred to as political, economic, and institutional. In this context "collective unconscious" has to do with crosscultural archetypes and elements of humanity not directly related to the external social and cultural milieu.

The notions of Religious, Political, Economic, and Psychological "Man" are in conflict with one another. That conflict is central to the cultural discontinuity in the Western world that has been evident through much of the twentieth century. The perception of discontinuity is itself a powerful source of the widespread feeling of anxiety, along with other causes of anxiety: economic injustice, the lack of a sense of community, global tensions and the threat of nuclear war, rampant hedonism demanding instantaneous gratification, alienation from work and occupation, downward mobility and social decline, loneliness, and interpersonal dissatisfaction. All of these are made more intense and more widespread by the discontinuity in culture. A lack of cultural continuity implies a lack of social stability. In terms of human perception and feeling the two are interchangeable, rather than one being cause and the other effect.

The agglomeration of population, the rise of democratization (which is only marginally an issue of governmental forms and representative institutions), the increase of pluralism, and the proliferation of taste cultures and a variety of so-called life-styles are social characteristics of modern Western life that have emerged and coalesced only during the last century. They *are* modern and contemporary life in the industrialized Western world. In their potential for variety they provide, on the one hand, an abundant source of independence, diversion, and opportunities to pursue happiness for those whom Robert Jay Lifton has described as modern Protean man. On the other hand, they have been the source of an increasing feeling of restlessness, a growing sense of discontinuity, and the spread of anxiety and anomie.

The twentieth century is not by any means the first epoch to experience cultural discontinuity. However, it may be the first in which discontinuity (which describes a surface effect) is accompanied by the deepening of perceptions of dislocation and meaninglessness. Aspects of apparent discontinuity, contradiction, and paradox may be apparent in any culture. To achieve such a situation seems, however, to have been the intent behind developments in the Western world since the Middle Ages. Whether it has been consciously recognized as such or not is another matter. The Western world's historic source of pride and accomplishment is also its primary source of recent and contemporary discontent. Tribalism, homogeneity, ritualism, and spiritual unity through communal forms have all been struggled against painstakingly and successfully since the fourteenth century. The most venerated individuals, movements, and works of creative imagination in Western civilization since the Renaissance have typically been at or near the forefront of this struggle. The spread of individual liberty, the promotion of cognitive processes, the debunking of obscurantism, superstition, and spirituality, however, have yielded mixed results. All of the varieties of the impulse to escape from freedom evident in the twentieth century—the most pernicious collective one having been Nazism—are rightly seen as attempts to evade the consequences of the course of Western civilization itself. Were this the case simply, the matter would be easier to handle than it is! It is really not a matter that can be accounted for by describing the desire for escape as an aberration. For Western civilization itself may be found wanting in its capacity to provide adequate satisfaction for deep human needs, which cannot simply be reasoned away. Hence, the double-edged sword of that happy accident we call civilization being in itself an enormous potential source of individual, and sometimes collective, discontent.

The notion of culture in the Western world was linked traditionally with the notion of standards. Standards are the provinces of elites, and elites function to exert sovereignty over them and conformity to them. The erosion and collapse of the traditional aristocracy in Europe, the rise of the middle classes in the nineteenth century, and the revolt of the masses in the twentieth century have challenged and overthrown much of the cultural domination of elites. This has been both a cause and a consequence of the transformations from patronage culture to commercial culture and the shift from cultural appreciation and connoisseurship to consumerism. The substitution of the influence of managers, technocrats, and professionals for the cultural will of aristocratic elites, the emergence of the national state as the temple of a shared popular mentality, and the replacement of theodicy by a variety of competing secular credos are all part of this legacy.

THE NATURE OF CULTURE AND THE WORK OF ART

The study of the peculiarity of "modern" institutions, or of those institutions shaped by "modernization," has been the central theme of sociological thought since its beginning. This topic is, indeed, the reason for sociology to have been established as a separate discipline late in the nineteenth century. The reconstruction of events and their causal motivations has been a central theme of historical writing since the late nineteenth century. The purpose of this essay is neither to describe and reevaluate modern institutions nor to reanalyze and reinterpret key events in Europe during the last hundred years. Rather, it is to pursue an inquiry beyond the phenomena of such institutions and events, to achieve a better understanding of certain imaginative works at the level of awareness, perception, and feeling.

This agenda is neither narrow nor marginal. Studied as such, institutions and events may reveal little or nothing of their relationship to human consciousness. Institutions and events are the actualization of specific perceptions, ambitions, prejudices, errors, and habits, not to mention calculations, impulses, and passions. Cultural works are the enactment of consciousness that springs from the same sources. Works of art are not only artifacts of the past, though of course they may be regarded as such. The surface qualities of cultural artifacts are related to events and institutions only obliquely. Their latent sources, always greater in volume and in depth than any surface actualization of them, are also related. The relationship of the actualizations to those things of the same order, which have come before or which come after them, is linear. The relationships between the unconscious sources behind them is associative. Moreover, the aesthetic theories of Robert Plant Armstrong inspire the conviction that the relationships of cultural works with institutions and events (even on the surface level) are associative. To study these relations in terms of origins, conscious influences, and direct connections is the project of traditional linear historiography. To encounter them associatively is a rejection of that historiography and marks an attempt not to misrepresent them as collective phenomena.

Cultural works are not merely the expression of someone's individual imagination. All humans have dreams, daydreams, and fantasies; these are not cultural works. Only when imagination and fantasy are rendered into form, imbued with meaning and value, and communicated do they become enactments of consciousness in a culture. Through this process they cease to be simply personal phenomena and become cultural ones. How this process is best understood—whether as the result of intuitive genius or virtuosity, external conditioning or influence, catering to a patron or a market, or of what is known in psychoanalysis as sublimation—is not the topic here. The element common to all cultural works is that they are projections of a dimension of experience into consciousness in such a way as to transcend the personalities and the material realities out of which they come.

Every mode of expression formalized in a given culture posesses primary social characteristics: where a particular kind of work is seen or heard, how it is displayed or presented, how its actualization is financed and criticized. All such modes of formalized expression also function ideologically; they mediate the lived relations between humans and their world. While works of art arise out of or are attuned to the material structure of social reality, they actualize into consciousness aspects of perception, sensitivity, and belief: the dynamic on which the actual workings of society are based.

With the increase of variety and discontinuity in the 20th century there has come about an expanded notion of culture. In common usage the word culture describes a broad range of creative works, tastes, habits, and preferences—including landscaping, architecture, eating, advertising, dress, speech and diction, spatial design, attitudes toward time, and so on. Here the reader will encounter no attempt to engage in anything resembling a comprehensive cultural history of Western Europe during the last hundred years. The focus instead is on works of the creative imagination in three modes of expression: narrative prose, dramatic writing, and motion pictures. They are interrelated by tradition; but, more importantly, they are all forms in which their own realities, embodying whole worlds in microcosm, are meant to be entered into by a reader or a viewer in a state of concentrated awareness.

They are works belonging primarily to a category called mimetic or representational. In them content is emphasized. They are not primarily decorative like pottery and weaving, and often painting. They depend upon referents to lived experience, though these may become blurred and tenuous. Unlike dance or music their affecting elements are not primarily kinetic.

Over against avant-gardism and experiments in the breaking down of traditional forms, the ascendancy of the representational narrative is an essential cultural element in the modern age. The main ideas and ideologies that define Western experience in the nineteenth and twentieth centuries are most empathically expressed first in prose fiction (novels) and subsequently in audiovocal and visual fiction (movies).

Traditional notions of culture have been challenged by, among other things, the democratization of public life and culture; notions of packaging and of markets for cultural objects; the advent of new forms of image communication, such as photography, cinematography, and video; and new media, such as radio and television. One response to that challenge—quite common to critics and historians of culture—is to delineate so-called high culture from popular, middle-brow, or mass culture. Such delineation, however, is not very valuable and is potentially misleading. Elite or less popular forms of expression are not necessarily better. Preferring movies to novels, or detective stories to psychological drama, or rock music to opera, is simply a matter of taste. Taste may be a function of age, or educational background, or economic status, and hence a matter of interest to sociologists. Taste, however, does not define the value or the meaning of a work. As the sociologist Herbert Gans has argued, fantasy, wish-fulfillment, and diversion are satisfied in myriad different ways for different people. The number of ways in which such satisfaction is offered has increased exponentially in the twentieth century. The capacity to reproduce a work (through printing, film reproduction, or recording) permits the work to be appreciated by ever-larger potential audiences.

The term "work of art" is a Western concept that describes a particular enactment of human thought and feeling into form. The term itself means little outside the Western world. To apply it to an African wood-carving, for example, is to impose, falsely, a specifically Western paradigm on it. This paradigm bears little relation to how such an object is actually created, perceived, and used in the culture in which it originates.

In the Western world, since the Renaissance, we have refined our approaches to understanding, evaluating, and criticizing what we call the work of art. "Genius," "beauty," and "linear development" are the coordinates for what have become abiding (and obsessive) concerns for questions of attribution, authenticity, originality, the search for personal style, and the analytical pursuit of the linear, historical, and surface determinates of why a work came to be. Instead, we need an anthro-psychology of the representational work itself. This psychology has nothing to do with the dehumanized precincts of experimentation, testing, and measurement that dominate present-day official academic practice of the discipline called psychology. Nor does it share a destiny with the Freudian or neo-Freudian interest in perspectives on the depth-psychological motives of individual creators of works of art. Rather, the approach here emphasizes the particular quality of consciousness that is enacted in every created work. Taking certain examples, it regards them as providing a basis for witnessing in specific forms the manifestation of shared collective psychic states and tendencies.

This approach emphasizes dealing with such works not as symbols exclusively, but as direct enactments of states of consciousness. The representational work of art stands for itself, in itself, and by itself. In opposition to the notion that the work of art simply symbolizes something else, this view emphasizes the integrity of the individual work, which will be engaged and witnessed in full recognition of its own consciousness (i.e., its being). In addition to positing its own consciousness, the representational work enacts states of consciousness that are collective. That is, each work manifests a dimension of experience as it is felt in a particular culture. No other object enacts the values of a culture so well as the work of art.

A culture is constituted of shared ideas and patterns of behavior. Through culture are filtered the experiences of both the collectivity and the individuals within it. The work of art is a special instance of articulating unformulated experience in the culture in the direction of consciousness. The work of art is not situated deterministically, but rather situates itself, in relationship to the relatively amorphous entity we call culture.

In this book selected works of narrative prose, dramatic writing, and movie-making will be regarded as created by a Western European, and not by a Frenchman, a German, an Italian, or an Englishman. Each work will be treated as making manifest a broadly shared experience as it is felt and perceived in the culture in which the work is created. This process of enactment will be regarded as the bringing to consciousness of the meanings of experience through their formalization in a work that is qualitatively representational. There is no interest here in what is commonly called the history of literature, or the history of drama, or the history of cinema: on the contrary, these mental constructs have been persistently bracketed out to permit engagement of the works in their own right as projections of consciousness. Hence, references to artistic movements, schools of thought, the examination of style as a specific category of creativity, and patterns of influence between specific works have been minimized.

Chapter Two
Individual Consciousness

THE THEOLOGIAN PAUL TILLICH has called the particular crisis of the modern age that of meaninglessness, which generates a peculiar anxiety with which man-as-consciousness has not been acquainted previously. Many other commentators have shared a similar opinion, including the poet W. H. Auden, who called the era immediately following the Second World War "The Age of Anxiety." Meaninglessness combined with anxiety might be thought of as the potent mixture that produces nihilism. The psychoanalyst Erich Fromm, who explored the social psychology of widespread feelings of emptiness and negation, concluded that the end product of those feelings would be a collective embrace of the irrational and destructive, as individuals sought to escape from the burdens of modern freedom, which caused our anxiety.

The fundamental issue confronting the making of meaning is the conflict between whether this project begins with the community or with the individual. Which starting point is chosen largely determines a wide range of issues: how the human condition, the nature of change, the course of history, and issues of right, sovereignty, ethics, and quite simply value, will be perceived. The conflict between our perceptions of either the "personal" or the "societal" being at the core of experience is a common element in modern Western thought and culture.

Philosophically, this conflict was present in aspects of Enlightenment thought by the mid-eighteenth century, as well as in Romanticism, which emerged by the end of that century. The thinkers and writers associated with both these established "movements" did not, in either case, close ranks with regard to this conflict. Out of the traditions of those two movements, and from the unresolved conflicts present in both of them respectively, eventually emerged a refined and sharpened opposition between the personal and the societal.

For purposes of simplicity that eventual occurrence may be linked with the names of two mid-nineteenth-century contemporaries, Karl Marx and Søren Kierkegaard. In his espousal of what he called "scientific" socialism and dialectial materialism, Marx was advancing the highest causes of Enlightenment rationalism, namely, universalization and standardization. Marx was at pains to distinguish his own analyses from the thinking of the romantic "utopian" socialists. He asserted that economic relationships are the basis of society, and declared the economic system to be determinant of consciousness within any given community. By contrast, Kierkegaard pushed to an extreme the romantic inwardness and self-positing that had produced the shift in which "consciousness" replaced "reason" as a central concern. In his rejection of the societal, Kierkegaard was exploring trenchantly the amorphous nature of human interiority, spirit, and intuitive knowledge. To these two fundamental ways of viewing experience, as they have carried down to our own day, the terms "neo-Marxian" and "neo-romantic" are frequently applied.

Both Marx and Kierkegaard, as well as the subsequent modern traditions of thought which they represent, were influenced by the German philosopher Georg Wilhelm Friedrich Hegel. Both were clearly beneficiaries of the Hegelian inheritance, although both were likewise dedicated to righting what they found wrong in Hegel. They used his thinking as a point of departure for their own, yet treated it surgically and critically.

Hegel, debatably, was the first serious and widely read philosopher of the modern age to shift the emphasis in Western thought from traditional categories of mind and substance to a more overriding concern called "consciousness." Hegel placed the emergence of consciousness in the awareness that grew from the coming to terms with opposites. It may be argued, however, that his own writings did not fully explore the dialectic of method and history so often ascribed to him; that clarification became the task of several of his immediate successors. Hegel anchored his notion of consciousness in rationality and purposefulness that proceeded through history as an expression of the spirit of the people (*Volk*) through the apparatus of the state. Marx, in his own words, set out to turn Hegel's thinking around 180 degrees: this meant the grounding of ideas in material realities by the positing of a dialectic in which the modes of production were distinguished from the forces of production. Those "forces" included social classes, whose characteristics were defined primarily in terms of collective economic shared-interest. The self-interest of the individual was, thus, subordinated to recognition of the conflicting material claims of classes in society, which stood in economic opposition to one another. Marx's version posited consciousness as a function of initial "class consciousness," and displaced Hegelian notions such as the "world historical spirit" in favor of a world historical process of material conflict.

Kierkegaard's departure from, and challenge to, Hegel was more extensive. Whereas Marx maintained the Hegelian commitment to reason and to optimism, Kierkegaard wholeheartedly embraced intuition and subjectivity. He was concerned with the human condition as individualized and as beginning spiritually and with interiority. He sought to inquire into the dialectial tension between human feeling or sensation and the transcendent source of human consciousness, the soul. He also spoke, however, of an "existential dialectic," and of thought's movement away from existence. By its nature, then, human consciousness was driven toward denial of the self in favor of communion with the cosmic.

From a contemporary vantage point, both Marx and Kierkegaard must be called prepsychological. This is so in spite of the fact that perhaps the best known of Kierkegaard's writings, *The Sickness unto Death* (1849), is subtitled "A Christian Psychological Exposition . . ." Today the issues of awareness and identity, which both Marx and Kierkegaard were exploring, although from entirely different and antithetical perspectives, are duly psychologized: that is, a new set of categories—beyond the language of sociology, political economy, theology, and philosophy—describes consciousness. Commonly, the fundamental question of consciousness is nowadays regarded as being as much a psychological issue as it is social or philosophical. Here we are choosing to argue that it is essentially cultural, culture being the vortex where thought and social reality intersect.

The divergence between societal and personal took on new meaning at the end of the eighteenth century. The challenges of romanticism to the narrow rationalism of Enlightenment thought established the disjointed cultural conflict of the modern age—defining it more clearly, perhaps, than C. P. Snow's notion that the discontinuity in contemporary Western culture is characterized by the widening split between the scientific and the humanistic or the literary.

Snow's widely spread nomenclature of the science/humanism split is a repetition of what is by now patterned in Western culture. Over the years we have sought to describe phenomena by reformulating the fundamental Platonic dualism of appearance and reality. Historically, that dualism seems a fundamental characteristic of Western culture. It might even be said that the dualistic split is the fundamental mythoform of Western civilization. This may have come to be so through the fact that above and beyond all else the West has been, ever since the barbarians were herded into the fold, Christian. Early Christianity took as its point of departure a neo-Platonism so firmly rooted in dualism that it subsequently influenced nearly every Western way of perceiving the world and humankind in it. Only with secularization does this begin to alter, but residual dualism has not yet been fully overcome.

With the growth of industry, the rise of modern institutions and bureaucracies, and the social changes called in sum "modernization," the lived reality of experience came to be felt increasingly as divided between the public and private. Neorationalism in its many forms has provided a basis for adjustments to changing social circumstances, technological change, growth of bureaucracy, and economic organization. By contrast, the neoromantic posture is suited to accommodating the rise of irrationalism, the flight into mythology, changes of psychological nature, and alterations in taste and life-style. The deeper question is whether evidence exists that the split between these two points of view might now be narrowing rather than widening. Do abstract art, the appearance of the "New" Left, or the new communications and information technologies reflect a state of consciousness, and hence a culture, that is breaking away from dualism, linearity, and discontinuity in the direction of a more tribalistic, oral, and integrated culture? Some embrace this possibility; the McLuhanites who survive do so religiously. Others cling to defending a venerated traditional culture, fearing that any traces of a new direction announce not the millenium, but rather the homogenized thought-controlled society of George Orwell's vision of a soulless technocracy, *1984*.

Speculation on such matters, however, belongs to another agenda. Here, attention is directed to the shifts in individual consciousness which are part of the response of Western culture to the course of historical development during the last century. The elaboration of the romantic quest for personal meaning and for spiritual understanding of the essence of human experience has, since 1870, been carried forward in light of a specific cultural and historical condition. In the guise of a parable, purporting to record the words of a madman who rushed into a village square bearing the news, Friedrich Nietzsche set forth the situation that, to a great extent, describes the fundamental situation of man's encounter with the human condition during the past hundred years:

> "Whereto has God gone?" he cried. "I shall tell you! We have slain him—you and I! All of us are his murderers! But how have we done this? How had we the means to drink the sea dry? Who gave us a sponge to efface the entire horizon? What were we about when we uncoupled this earth from its sun? Where is the earth moving to now? Where are we moving? Away from all suns? Are we falling continuously? And backward and sideways and forward in all directions? Is there still an above and below? Are we not wandering lost as through an upending void? Does vacant space not breathe at us? Has it not grown colder? Is there not perpetual nightfall and more night? Must we not light lanterns in the morning? Do we hear nothing of the gravediggers who are burying God? Is there no smell of divine putrefication?—the gods also decompose! God is dead! God stays dead! And we have killed him! How shall we comfort ourselves, who are killers above all killers? The holiest and mightiest that the world has hitherto possessed has bled to death under our knives—who shall wipe that blood off us?" [George Steiner, trans., 1967]

Proclaiming the event was no great news to the nineteenth-century intellectual establishment. Decades before, numerous thinkers—including Feuerbach, Comte, Mill, Stendhal, Büchner, Flaubert, and, of course, Marx—had made similar observations. Nonetheless, it was the Nietzschean description that eventually seized the Western imagination.

The death of God is not the same as loss of faith. The former is concerned with the modern theme of secularization only marginally. The death of God, in the first instance, was caused by the ascendancy of science and the fact that, in Nietzsche's view, science had no place for God. But God survived in human value systems long after science had moved to the forefront of thought. The death of God marked an interior condition of the Western mind, and one that was fraught with dissonance and contradiction. It produced an epistemological crisis, or, put more simply, a crisis of meaning—and a central and irrevocable one.

The central contradiction that defined the crisis of meaning caused by the felt reality of the death of God was paralelled by the society that emerged after 1870 in places that were already industrialized. The three decades from 1870 to 1900 are called sometimes an "age of materialism." Open to question as all such appellations are, this nomenclature seems relatively appropriate to the epoch. With the accelerating rise of the bourgeoisie, the increasing currency of nineteenth-century liberal ideas, a sudden increase in the complexity of industry and the instruments of investment capitalism, the economic and social complexion of Europe was changing. This was accompanied by a rise in nationalism and a cult of national self-consciousness. In turn the ethos of the age was projected beyond Europe in a paroxysm of rapid and rapacious imperialistic expansion undertaken by the Western nations across the globe. This imperialism can be accounted for on the basis of economic ambition, but neither as a general phenomenon nor in its specific instances can it thus be adequately explained. In retrospect, the imperialist scramble, which often was a considerable gamble, was a collective pathology reflecting anxiety that raged beneath the relatively smooth surface of smugness, self-confidence, and pride that characterized the shared mentality of the age. That mentality took satisfaction in the rise of science and the increasing influence of positivism. That science was not, as yet, fully accountable for the murder of God, though its complicity might be suggested to anyone sifting through the evidence. When Nietzsche recorded the event, the conflict between religion and science that sprang from Charles Darwin's theory of evolution was in its initial stages. That conflict went back much farther, however: in the eighteenth century both David Hume and Immanuel Kant had set science in opposition to religion. In fact, Kant had already been credited by Heinrich Heine with doing away with God.

The sweeping to prominence of scientific ideas and thinking, however, related in a convoluted manner to what Nietzsche was describing. Evolutionary ideas themselves had little to do with the materialism of the age that dominated the end of the nineteenth century, though they were at times exploited in defense of it. The potential for technological exploitation of this particular line of biological science was negligible. Genetics, and discoveries in it and in related fields, became exploitable only later.

What was important about the materialist age was the industrial exploitation of only certain scientific ideas—not of evolutionary theory, for example, but of geology, which was important for the development of petrochemicals, or, even more directly, chemistry itself. This necessitated a shift from labor-intensive to capital-intensive industry. That shift did many things, not the least of which was to undermine the efficacy of the entreprenurial initiative of the energetic individual. Science and technology requirng an extensive economic structure began replacing the spirit and initiative of the independent entrepreneur.

While the bourgeois, the so-called cornerstone of modern capitalist industrial society, remained in general conventionally religious, the sort of society that they were building was rife with elements displacing God from the center of things. The society which was growing and becoming triumphant was rooted in a materialism that necessarily undermined any notion of the transcendent. This predicament underscored what might be called (borrowing Nietzschean language, but giving to it a slightly different twist) a central "life-lie" of modern middle-class society. The triumph of a society based upon materialism, which is credited with changing so many aspects of life and culture, cannot change them without having consequences of a profound nature on human consciousness.

To call the inability or unwillingness to embrace the consequences of this predicament a "lie" is imprecise. Strictly speaking, a "lie" is a willful and intentional untruth. In this regard, nearly any depth-psychological perspective on self-delusion calls "intent" into question. Whether a lie or an unintentional self-deception, this collective delusion is evident—evident, it must be said, with exceptions. It is simply a matter of observation that much received, shared, and mainstream thinking in Western culture does not come to terms with this issue. This is documented in the mental gymnastics performed by numerous men and women whose religiosity might be called socially conventional. Moreover, it is evinced in the historical record of the vast and almost complete accommodation of Christian churches and sects to modernization and its many implications.

Nietzsche hinted at, but never precisely elucidated, the connectedness of the event of God's death to the processes of social change and modernization evident even in his own time. The rise of the middle classes and the extension of elements of democratization and modern pluralism were aspects of his age that Nietzsche condemned. This makes him a highly problematic figure even today for anyone committed ideologically to defense of one or another brand of liberal democracy. On that score, Nietzsche is more palatable to some by dint of his attack on bourgeois philistinism. However, once their political, economic, or social status improves even slightly, even the lower classes in Western Europe have shown a penchant for feeding on distinctively bourgeois attitudes and norms, hence bringing down Nietzsche's critique on them, too.

Nietzsche was not attacking the bourgeois for their exploitative control of the modes of industrial production and their avaricious profit-seeking. He attacked their philistinism exclusively. But to what end did he attack it? The issue goes beyond any mere critique of bourgeois smugness and conventionality to the erosion of moral sovereignty in society ushered in by the rise of the middle classes. This erosion of elite moral sovereignty in most of Europe meant socially what God's death meant epistemologically—namely, the elimination of His authority over the universe and over human consciousness. What characterized the rise of the bourgeois, and subsequently the rise of the masses at the time of the First World War, was the erosion of a willingness to exert sovereignty, as expressed specifically in the posture of accepting moral responsibilities.

Historically the European aristocracy had exerted just such moral authority. In England and perhaps in France its capacities to do so began to weaken perceptibly, both from outside challenges and from decay within its own ranks, by the mid-eighteenth century. Once that process of decline commenced it spread and soon became the central social issue of European history. As a theme it dominated nineteenth-century European life, and was not fully exhausted until the end of the First World War. Historians long have debated the rate of the aristocracy's decline and just when its demise was final. The nineteenth-century historian Daniel Halévy, for example, dated the end of the *"notables"* (in his book of that name) specifically to 1881!

Culturally, in terms of the phenomena of representational works of art or enactment, the aristocracy had lost any real dominance over them by the early nineteenth century. The ascendancy of the novel, the burgeoning of print-culture, and the spread of literacy (nearly total in Western Europe by the 1880s, except for Italy and the Iberian Peninsula) occurred in isolation from aristocratic patronage of production, or aristocratic domination of form or content, or aristocratic control of the educational apparatus strictly for its own ends. Culturally, in terms of the perception of the aristocracy's decline—let us say aristocracy's death—the theme itself spread widely in representational works after 1870. It was a relatively common one up until the First World War, after which general concern with it declined and what concern remained became increasingly identifiable as conservative in temperament.

With the death of God and the death of the European aristocracy, questions of sovereignty, authority, and the legitimate exertion of will in culture, morals, and values have become central to the twentieth-century experience. A common response by thinkers and writers is to use representational works of art to encourage individuals to accept a measure of such responsibility in order to fill the vacuum.

In the late nineteenth century that moral vacuum was first confronted in representational works describing the undermining of individual responsibility through middle-class conventionality, hypocrisy, and arbitrary social tensions—a confrontation at the heart of those literary and dramatic works now called naturalistic. The most trenchant of the naturalistic dramas are perhaps those by the playwrights Henrik Ibsen, August Strindberg(especially his early plays), Gerhard Hauptmann, and Franz Wedekind. Emile Zola's numerous novels are perhaps as complete a reflection of naturalistic principles as have been created. Zola attempted to subject fictional narrative to what he considered to be scientific techniques. He produced long and detailed passages of description and observation, which were meant to be underscored by an abiding strain of social commentary and criticism. One of the most powerful naturalistic writers in the English language was Thomas Hardy. In *Jude the Obscure* and *Tess D'Urbevilles*, for example, Hardy captures the complexities of social contradictions, hyprocrisy, and the weight of conventionality in simple, homely language and with forceful descriptive passages.

Naturalistic novels and plays, however, were severely limited with regard to their capacity to make manifest the complex dimensions of individual consciousness. Partly because of their reliance on descriptions of the coarseness and brutality of social customs and conventions, naturalist works seem often to caricature—rather than to characterize—the hypocrisies of late-nineteenth-century society. Naturalism as a style, or as a conceptual *coda* within which the representational work is achieved, ran the risk of over-emphasis on surface detail. This inclination toward the accretion of description, the exaggerations of social caricature, and the attention to detail was later found wanting. For example, existential concerns, for the depth psychology and interiority of alienation, were unsatisfied in naturalism's glib assertion that individual crisis was caused almost exclusively by social pressures. Subsequently, too, those leftists who perceived individual liberation as coming through radical changes in the basic political and economic structures of society found inadequate the naturalistic obsession with superficial critiques of social injustices.

In contrast to naturalistic modes, Joseph Conrad's novel *Heart of Darkness* (1901) explores uprootedness and homelessness: it embraces the meaninglessness, anxiety, and moral exhaustion in which modern individual consciousness is born. Told through a character's voice, it does not engage individual consciousness with the force of first-person narration or the objectivity of a third-person voice. What Marlow describes appears to be an adventure set in Central Africa. The true adventure here, however, is the protagonist's encounter with forces of enormous spiritual power. Kurtz personifies the high-mindedness of the aggressive defender of Western civilization, the post-religious materialist and scientific zealot. He is undermined spiritually and emotionally by his encounter with the native and the primitive. This force, over against Kurtz's will, proves to be more powerful than anything that still resides in the culture of the West and that has been translated into his individuality. Tribalism and magic are so overwhelming that the veneer of Western civilization offers no adequate defenses against them. Kurtz's encounter with them calls into question not simply the surface qualities of that Western civilization but the nature of the Western self. For if in a given situation the assumptions of a civilization no longer support the individual adequately he is thrown back upon his own meager means. In a literal sense, Kurtz's situation is rare. In its essence, however, it has become increasingly common; it is a mode of being or doing in which the ego-self surrenders as the spiritual core of one's own culture collapses.

Kurtz's dilemma is portrayed as a dramatic actualization of exhaustion resulting in the giving over of oneself to primitive, irrational, and alien forces. Kurtz lives through a sickness unto death that draws him from his moorings, the assumptions of his materialist civilization. The native culture presents him with a challenge that is distasteful yet, at the same time, seductive. Kurtz is confronted with nothing less than the imminent possibility of the extinction of the self. The crude words of the native who announces to Marlow, "Mr. Kurtz he dead," bear the reasonance of that simpleness of finality that is difficult for the modern Western world to accept. Kurtz accepts his own sacrifice to something taboo but instinctually alluring. He has embraced it, accepting all the consequences.

A good parallel figure to Kurtz in narrative fiction is the protagonist of Thomas Mann's *Death in Venice* (1911). Gustav von Aschenbach is an acclaimed writer, dedicated to the rigors of discipline and accomplishment, a pillar of propriety and restraint, and above all a man of reason and judgment. He is moved by what is only a vague *Wanderlust* to travel from his home in Munich to Venice for an off-season vacation.

At first, this seems innocent and unproblematic enough. As Aschenbach arrives, however, images of alienation and decay confront him. Soon after taking a room in a grand Venetian hotel, he becomes infatuated from a distance with a young Polish boy named Tadzio who is staying there with his family. Giving in to his voyeurism, Aschenbach begins stalking the boy. He does so awkwardly, with an almost infantile air. Yet Aschenbach grows weary before the reader's eyes. At the same time, as the layers of his decorum are peeled away, he becomes marginally more reflective and perceptive about his own condition, with vanity filling in the rest of his dislocated psychic space. He can neither be direct with Tadzio nor hold his impulses in check by ignoring Tadzio and going about other business.

Only after Aschenbach puts together the shreds of evidence that a plague has struck Venice does he come near enough to the boy to see him closely. Tadzio has pock-marked skin and a sickly complexion. Aschenbach fails to leave the city—through his lack of will to do so, as well as because of problems with shipping his baggage—is taken ill, and dies. His death is reported in major newspapers across Europe.

The historian Rudolph Binion has described Aschenbach's dilemma as being that of a man who discovers that he is living beyond his own moral means. That discovery may be paralleled by a mentality spreading in the European intelligensia on the eve of World War One, though not yet dominant.

Aschenbach has traveled only as far as Venice and not outside Europe. Yet when he first fantasized about leaving Munich before actually departing, his mind's eye conjured up images of milk-white floating flowers, knotted bamboo, and the glowing eyes of a crouching tiger. Moreover, the plague that grips Venice and kills Aschenbach originated, we learn, on the banks of the Ganges river in India. Aschenbach's plight is an instance of regression, much as is Kurtz's. This psychological suggestion symbolizes an aspect of the cultural condition that emerged in Europe in the ten to fifteen years before the outbreak of war in 1914. A simpler line of discussion starts with the fact of dislocation as precipitating the fatal crisis of both these characters. Kurtz is undone by the encountering of spiritual forces from outside and beyond himself. Aschenbach is the victim of his own inner impulses, which, catalyzed by another person who attracts him from afar, rise and overwhelm him. In both instances the emotional and moral equilibrium of the protagonists is torn apart by their encounters with the foreign, the alien, and that which is of another place and another world. It is as if the assumptions and standards of Western civilization can stand scant challenge; as if European man can endure little disquieting or unsettling confrontation with that which is different.

Both works—*The Heart of Darkness* directly and *Death in Venice* obliquely—may be connected with the theme of European imperialism. They might be thought of as enactments of the underside of the imperialist triumphs: explorations of the tenuous and feeble set of self-assured values with which Europe had projected itself upon the rest of the world. In this way they might be considered as tortured explorations in the self-deception and eventual self-destructiveness of a civilization. Such consideration ignores, however, the more deeply pervasive and widely felt dimension of experience from which they arise: namely, the displacement and uprootedness that were spreading in industrialized, urbanized, and modernized Western society.

To say this is not to suggest that these images of enactment coincide with precision to the actual social development of Europe. By the beginning of this century, however, the patterns of dislocation, uprootedness, and intellectual and moral homelessness were already evident; and all this meshed with the cosmic change occasioned by God's death.

These two pre–World War One works explore aspects of the emerging crisis of individual consciousness from slightly different perspectives. They are typical of many twentieth-century works in which the individual goes outside of a customary civilization, social order, or ambiance, to encounter there a challenge that brings the individual's self, and all its constitutive self-assumptions, into question. Such a situation may be misconstrued as a simple suggestion that the individual runs terrible risks in any departure from his or her own cultural place and social role. Such a misconstrual leads to the misinterpretation of this theme as patently conservative, conveying the impossibility of moving beyond one's own social stratum or place in the relative order of things.

Situations like this have been enacted in numerous works of creative imagination. One that is especially rich in elements akin to those in both *Heart of Darkness* and *Death in Venice* is the motion picture *The Passenger* (1974). Produced by a British firm, with dialogue in English, directed by the Italian Michelangelo Antonioni, set in Africa and in several places on the European continent, with the American actor Jack Nicholson in the lead role, the making of the film reflects the narrowing of distinctions between specific national cultures.

In *The Passenger* the main character, David Locke, is a British television journalist on assignment in an African country. He is reporting on an insurgent rebel movement. In a small, out-of-the-way hotel where he is staying, Locke discovers the body of another Englishman of his acquaintance named Robertson, who has died of a heart attack. Immediately, without explanation or reflection, Locke decides to assume Robertson's identity. As he is moving the body to his own room and doctoring Robertson's passport by replacing the photo in it with his own, Locke recollects their first meeting several days before. This is no flashback, but rather a visualization connecting the present moment and that incident of the recent past joined by memory. It is laced with visual deceptions, just as actual individual memory is laced with deceptions of a personal, cultural, or chronological sort. Robertson is there physically with Locke, alive and talking—yet, simultaneously, his dead body is on the floor. This is a recreation of the earlier occasion of their actual meeting, with a tape recording of their conversation that Locke had made surreptitiously played during the recollection/recreation as an aide-memoire.

This scene portrays the subtleties and deceptions that have increasingly come to surround and inform the exploration of individual consciousness. Identifying Robertson's body as his own, Locke ships it to England. Then he commences on an odyssey that adheres faithfully to meetings listed in a date book he has discovered in Robertson's effects. Locke soon discovers himself keeping the schedule of a gun-runner for the rebels. He never really connects with all the deep psychological and ideological aspects of his new identity and role. Nonetheless, he never wavers toward abandoning a living out of this destiny that has come his way accidently, but which he has chosen.

His wife and his producer in London come to suspect that he may still be alive. By then Locke has arrived in Barcelona, where he meets a young woman. He has not known her before, but he has seen her before; so he thinks, and so thinks the viewer. Knowing that he is pursued both by his wife and by agents of the African government to whose opponents he supplies arms, Robertson leaves Barcelona with the young woman. As they ride in an open convertible through the countryside she asks him what he is running from. He tells her to turn; she does, and the screen is filled with the long, narrow, empty, tree-lined road down which they are speeding. He is fleeing from nothing, simply from what was.

In a small village, where they take a room, Locke is assassinated by the government agents while his female companion is outside. His wife arrives with the Spanish police, is shown the dead man on the bed, and tells the police that she never knew that man. The female companion enters and says that yes, she knew him!

Locke is an updated equivalent to Kurtz in several ways: he has gone to Africa, albeit contemporary-style, armed with recorders and cameras, in search of interviews and information. He does not succumb to the power of anything spiritual that he encounters. Instead, unwittingly, he becomes an agent for the liberation struggle there. He has linked himself on the surface with the Third World by playing out his role as a supplier of firepower (i.e., technology). His giving up of himself to some force outside himself is akin to Aschenbach's dilemma, yet also decidedly different. Locke has chosen; Aschenbach is compelled by inner forces. Locke has become another person; Aschenbach has given in to the deeper, darkling, and repressed elements of his own self. Yet Locke is not in bad faith. Emotionally his choice and his living out of his new being are authentic. He accepts the consequences of that choice; overtly he could have abandoned the role of Robertson at any point. He has, then, an exit, although beneath the surface of the narrative one feels that in essence he did not. For reasons never revealed in the enactment itself, he elects to live out Robertson's datebook and his life.

These very qualities of open-endedness are characteristic of the nature of the shift in individual consciousness during the twentieth century. Locke's situation is precipitated neither by depth-psychological determinants, nor by an external factor identified in the narrative.

The interest here in identity and role, it hardly need be mentioned, coincides with the relatively recent sociological and popularized psychological concerns for both in the Western world. Alongside the theme of communication, identity and role are probably the most widely acknowledged categories in which the crisis of selfhood is understood in the West today. Overtly, these categories are more fully developed in their social ramifications and more directly connected with social factors than those more amorphous qualities of alienation that preceded them earlier in the century. The naturalistic emphasis on external restrictions and culture-bound denials are here abandoned, pointing to the preoccupation with them as dated. Locke encounters no repressive social order in his wanderings. He encounters no frustration from the young woman he happens upon in the building in Barcelona—she befriends him, sleeps with him, goes off with him, and after he is dead loyally attests to knowing him as well.

Another motion picture, *Hiroshima, mon amour,* directed by Alain Resnais from a Marguerite Duras screenplay in 1959, is a variation in the enactment of the discovery of self when an experience outside the individual's own milieu serves as a trigger. Kurtz, Aschenbach, and Locke all encountered, in a specific condition of displacement, a spontaneous and overwhelming impulse in the direction of being taken over by a force greater than themselves. The female protagonist of *Hiroshima,* a French actress nearing middle age, is not named in the narrative until at the end her lover calls her by the name of the town in France where she grew up (Nevers). She experiences all along the welling up of that which is repressed within her. This repressed material is specific. As a young girl, she had an affair with a German soldier of the occupation forces in her town. He was killed by Partisans. She was found kneeling near his body, and after the liberation she was humiliated and ostracized until one day she was sent off to Paris by her parents.

The actress is a member of a production company filming a movie about world peace on location in Hiroshima. This much of the narrative coincides with the relatively widespread concern over atomic weapons in Europe in the late 1950s, which translated into protests and manifestations under the banner of "Ban the Bomb." She meets a Japanese architect in a tea house the day before she is to return to Paris. Their liaison leads her to tell him the story of her experience with the German soldier and all its consequences. She reveals this to him, a relative stranger, having previously recounted it to no one before. It is a rambling confession, a baring of psychological scars. Their adultery (for both she and the architect have spouses), a point of narrative tension in many mimetic works, here does not matter. The conventional taboo being violated is ignored, as are any overt references to racial difference as a point of friction.

The film depicts directly memory, recollection, and reconstruction, pointing to an adventure in retrieval and self-recognition that barely skirts being psychoanalytical. What the protagonist retrieves is not material bedded deeply in the unconscious, but a recollection that she has consciously held beneath the surface level. By comparison, Aschenbach's interior revelation of homosexual impulses, with which he cannot come to terms, is closer to the processes and concerns of psychoanalysis proper, even though *Death in Venice* was published while Freud, in Vienna, was still only experimenting with analysis, which did not become culturally established until after the First World War.

In *Hiroshima* it is a specific political context, and the further suggestions of other such contexts beyond the immediate one in view of the camera, that underlies the heroine's revelation. Perhaps it is the enormity of trying to grasp the dropping of the atomic bomb on Hiroshima, the coming of what is called the "Atomic Age" (as if it could be described so simply and glibly with the same sort of term we have used to characterize other periods and epochs), that precipitates her turning inward as much as toward the man across the teahouse table from her. Their relationship, after all, is more significant in its empathy and curiosity than in its passion and romance.

Hiroshima is a visually dynamic exploration of memory. This is especially true of a sequence in which the actress wanders the streets of Hiroshima late at night, the façades of the neon-lit buildings being replaced sequentially and directly by images of Nevers in 1944. The exploration of memory, the challenge of reconstructing it and making meaning and a rediscovery of self-in-authenticity from its traces, is one of the more striking and pervasive elements of twentieth-century narrative and fiction in Western Europe.

At one level, the growth in the Western world of an audience for biography and autobiography is documentable. On another, there is the rise of psychoanalytical belief and practice, scientific as well as popular interest in dreams, and a widespread concern that defies precise labeling for the awareness of self in terms of the remembrance of experiences out of which one has come. These concerns relate to a turning inward, to an interest in self, different both in kind and in degree from what previous societies in the West have experienced.

Individualism in the nineteenth century, after all, was an entirely different matter. Smugness, self-confidence, and the forceful projection of one's persona upon the world—underwritten by ample doses of rationalism and liberalism—have little to do with the search for self and the reorientation of individual consciousness in the twentieth century. Earlier links have to be traced to sources such as Jean-

Jacques Rousseau's *Confessions* (written in the mid-eighteenth century) or to specific works of the Romantic era. Georges Stendhal's personal search for identity, or Georg Büchner's surpassing nonperson Woyzeck (who is updated in Werner Herzog's 1978 movie of that name) are good examples.

In representational works by the first years of the twentieth century the turning inward and the pursuit of memory became less than rare. In this vein, Rainer-Maria Rilke's *Notebooks* (1910), Richard Beer-Hofmann's *Georg's Death* (1900), Andre Gide's *The Immoralist* (1902), Luigi Pirandello's *The Late Matthia Pascal* (1904), and Italo Svevo's *The Conscience of Zeno* (1923) merit mention. Though overworked in critical and historical treatments, Marcel Proust's *Remembrance of Things Past* illustrates well the emerging attempt at depicting what might be called the memory-time-self continuum. Completed in volumes appearing between 1913 and 1923, the work commences with *Swann's Way* (published just before the First World War). From that volume on, the overt social commentary in Proust's series embraces the frequently surveyed terrain of the triumph of the aggressive middle classes over a decaying aristocracy. The essence of Proust's undertaking, however, is his approach to narration itself. While fragmentation and disconnectedness had been either implied or suggested in many works, *Remembrance of Things Past* directly embraces disorder, randomness, and the processes of time.

The narrator-protagonist himself is the only genuine focus of unity throughout the work. The veritable enactment of meaning through personal retrieval or rediscovery is the work of a single mind and spirit engaged in the reexploration of its own personal history through all the myriad associative links to each and every intellectual and sensory tracing left in memory. To make these manifest is to reconstruct the universe of the self through its sensitive reordering.

Here there is a playing with the notion of art itself in light of the process of reconstruction. There is a self-consciousness that borders on solipsism. Were *Remembrance* to be first published today it would likely be greeted with the criticism presently in vogue that it is "self-indulgent." Yet central perhaps to *Remembrance of Things Past* is the ironic tension that exists in juxtaposing the communication between people that is superficial and tinged with emptiness against the interior monologue of the conscious self with the inner recesses of memory. There is here an exploration of the role of the senses in memory: hearing, taste, smell, sight. So far as literary tradition evinces a point of departure for understanding this quest, it might be called a kind of super-realism. The inner absorption and ordering of experience supersede the exploration of external reality. In *Remembrance of Things Past*, in convoluted fashion, that dimension of experience that may be called uprootedness is portrayed. It is not similar, but parallel, to the writings in German of Franz Kafka, a Czech, which are contemporary to Proust's publications in France.

Kafka, at least at one level, can be more easily interpreted than Proust by many readers. His is an exploration of dislocation of the individual from his surroundings through a nearly classic enactment of the condition called alienation. His writings are excursions into disconnectedness and disassociation. His protagonists—mostly autobiographical, of course—find themselves in situations of absurdity and labyrinthine complexity, confronted by a world in which their possibilities of constructing contextual connecting links of meaning are nil. The Kafkaesque (for the term has become widely spread in popular Western parlance since World War Two) is a vision in which reconstruction is impossible. It is an encounter with the underside of the self, a loss of awareness that borders on the pathological. Initially, Kafka's writings were taken to be the tortured and idiosyncratic working off of tension rooted in aberration and disorientation. Only when several figures in France (atheist existentialists, to label them conveniently) managed to extend the interpretation of Kafka's works did they take on the new meaning and significance that they have had for readers since World War II. During the 1920s and 1930s they appeared, even to those sensitive to them in positive ways, more as case studies in tortured alienation bordering on insanity, than as compelling enactments of a consciousness attuned to the radical shifts in character and content of personal existence since the death of God. Perhaps it is only in light of that which culminates at the end of the 1930s and during the course of the Second World War—nazism, Hiroshima, the Holocaust, the Gulag—that this Kafkaesque vision takes on a fullness of meaning. Stalin's purge trials and the revelations of the Gulag, Hitler's extermination camps and the eventual exploring of the banality of evil, and Truman's order to bomb Hiroshima and Nagasaki are preconditions of Kafka's seeming singularity of vision catching up with Western humankind—or perhaps the reverse, Western humankind catching up with *The Metamorphosis*, *The Trial*, and *The Castle*. Only after 1945 can the mechanisms of destruction, inhumanity, and murder en masse be understood as placing the individual in a situation differing both in kind and in degree from any previously known. That is the perception of the individual victimized beyond human control and understanding—even beyond the control and understanding of those who are in charge.

Yet it should not be assumed mistakenly that the Kafkaesque marks the main, or even the dominant, mode of individual consciousness in modern Western experience. The direction of reconstruction, the superrealism of Proust, has shown vitality if not ascendancy. The novels of the Irishman James Joyce, who spent most of his adult life in self-chosen exile on the European continent, are an example. In *Ulysses* (1922) and *Finnegan's Wake* (1937) the reader encounters a reconstruction that cuts across the varieties of experience, that expands the details of interconnectedness in exploration, and that is, at times, earthy, riotous, erotic, and humorous. Experience, impression, and meaning are explored in the memory and being of each individual. Here, too, the sense of place is important, although displacement from it is not the central idea. Here, too, the rhythm of life is explored.

Rhythm is a category of experience that has become more pronouncedly significant in individual consciousness in the twentieth century. Yet even where it is more obvious and ostensibly unencumbered in human experience—namely, in music—rhythm is indefinable. Yet it is ever-present, from the noise of traffic (both human and vehicular) in urban centers to the sense that we all have of recognizing someone's walk down a hallway even before we have seen him or her. A passage in Proust describes a boyhood recollection of knowing that it was his aunt, rather than anyone else in the household, mounting the stairway as he heard her footsteps distantly from inside his closed room. Joyce's writing explores rhythm and tempo more than anything else. Perhaps it was the undefinable nature of this epiphenomenon of human individuality, so indefinable even in its pristine musical presentation, that led Joyce to the breaking down of language itself. Joyce's writing eventually struggled beyond word association and word play to the construction of new words, new language—words and language that seem, on the surface, to be inaccessible. Joyce's radical assaults upon language are to some observers only a perverse demonstration of virtuosity for its own sake, a pushing of the literary (Western culture's most venerated and potentially durable mimetic form) in the directions of dehumanization and nihilistic autodestructive anti-art. On the other hand, the links are evident between Joyce's goals and the concerns of the Vienna

School, Ludwig Wittgenstein, logical positivism, and phenomenology for language and its incapacities to describe or to reconstruct the essence of experience. This perception of the failure of the word influences all sorts of enactments of experience from stream-of-consciousness writing to the *choisiste* project of a radical situationality that emerged in the 1950s with the writings of Michel Butor, Alain Robbe-Grillet, and Nathalie Saurraute. Beyond that *choisme* is the painful portrayal of protagonists who demonstrate by gesture and a stylized frustration the inability either to communicate with others or to externalize pain, as in Rainer Werner Fassbinder's films *The Merchant of Four Seasons* (1971) and the *Bitter Tears of Petra von Kant* (1972).

These directions in twentieth-century culture, enactments of a dimension of experience in the ambient and environing world that becomes more commonly shared and agreed upon emotionally, can be connected with the tempo of urban life, the impact of technologies upon human sensoria, and geographical and social dislocations that increasingly are the underside of the highly evident phenomenon of mobility. It would be a mistake, however, to assume that the tracings of linkage account for anything causally. In the representational works that best characterize individual consciousness in the twentieth century, the themes appear before the phenomenon becomes widespread in social experience. This recognition allows of many interpretations. Two of the most prominent are: (1) to regard the novels, plays, or movies as springing from idiosyncratic individual sources and then gaining staying-power and becoming spiritually accessible as events and social processes caught up with what they enacted; or (2) to regard the crisis itself to which these works are addressed, and to which modern and contemporary individuals have become increasingly sensitive, as caused by intellectual-emotional-spiritual dislocation to which the later-appearing concrete aspects of dislocation through technology and increased mobility have lent credence.

Depth exploration into the individual self and its interiority might be understood as the twentieth century extension, in a radically new direction, of the pursuit of human wholeness. The notion of the Renaissance Man, the individual whose knowledge, understanding, and wisdom extends across the full reaches of human learning and inquiry, had become by mid-eighteenth century the expanded category suggested by the idea of Encyclopedic Man. This venerated goal of wholeness through comprehension became widely popularized throughout the nineteenth century and became for a while a kind of cultural cause. This cause reached its acme in the triumph of science and the rush to attach all forms of knowing and inquiry to a basis in scientific method. In this anthropologized empiricism were the outlines for understanding social and economic processes, competition and inequality, human aggression and imperialism, individualism and war. In the development of wholly different perspectives on individual consciousness in the twentieth century, attention has shifted from the goal of a comprehensive horizontal individual claim upon knowledge and understanding toward what might be called a vertical seeking into oneself for ever-deeper layers of meaning unearthed from the recesses of human memory—personal, racial, and historical.

The conflict between extensions of the notion of the rational encyclopedic self as the highest attainment of being human (moderated, of course, by certain practical adjustments to the exponential increase in the sheer volume of what there is to know) and the romantic notion of introspection into one's own singular selfhood characterizes the contemporary discontinuity in Western thought and culture. Stream of consciousness, interior monologue, and a variety of related perspectives enter into the deepest recesses of the individual, the self. This parallels the rise of psychoanalysis and the range of clinical and scientific perspectives on the self viewed from the point of view of a depth psychology. Nonetheless, the quest to enact and manifest this sensibility in representational works is not merely a subsidiary and secondary offshoot of the mainstream concerns of psychoanalysis and various forms of modern psychology. Sometimes it may seem so. For to many it looks as if analysts and artists share a common mission. Whatever the links between analysis and self-reflective art, the one is not demonstrably caused by the other. Viewed culturally, this quest predates (surely back to the early-nineteenth-century romantics, or at least back to a figure such as Søren Kierkegaard) the institutionalization of modern clinical psychology at the end of the 1870s, the advent of Freudianism and psychoanalysis, and the subsequent combinations that yield the panoply of introspective, solipsistic, narcissistic, neoromantic, mystical, analytical, and phenomenological approaches to the self.

That these varying perspectives have appeared in the Western experience more or less concurrently lends credibility to that pitfall in intellectual and cultural history, the notion of a *Zeitgeist*, or "spirit of the times." Such a notion results from a phantasm which takes contemporaneous appearances, especially when the evidence of direct and concrete influence of one figure or idea upon another is lacking, to reveal that somehow ideas, perspectives, and notions were in the air. Nothing is in the air except the chemical elements that compose the earth's atmosphere, plus those that are added to it by the advance of technology (i.e., pollutants). Notions of a spirit of the times and of ideas fluttering in the breeze are a liability. Yet it is undeniable that the transfer of ideas, perceptions, and points of view has altered dramatically in the twentieth century. It may be the case in this century that normally the ideas and perceptions of most individuals (including highly sophisticated and learned ones) derive not from direct encounter with the original source of their articulation, but rather from a secondary source. The issue may be confused by the proliferation of the media (both print and electronic), the rise of mass education (staffed by veritable armies of interpreters), and the rapid popularization and dissemination of insights that have originated in the lonely quest of individual minds. Taken together they yield a very different coloration to intellectual and cultural life in the twentieth century. Still, there is no excuse for confusing an issue of communication and the sociology of knowledge with idealist conjectures about a spirit of the times.

A form of narrative representationalism has arisen since the 1920s that is unabashedly psychoanalytical in its character and content. It is a mistake, however, to regard the dimensions of individual consciousness portrayed culturally as shot through with psychoanalytical import. Psychoanalytic categories and methods have proven more valuable in accounting for and adding to an understanding of certain depictions of individual consciousness than in causing, or directly influencing, them. This generalization is far more accurate for Western Europe than for the United States. In the United States since World War II, the enacting of images of determinant factors of a psychoanalytical sort has been far more common in novel, drama, and film—from J. D. Salinger's *Catcher in the Rye* (1951) to Edward Albee's *Who's Afraid of Virginia Woolf* (1962) to *Ordinary People*, a film directed by Robert Redford in 1979.

In Western Europe, the bent to emulate and enact the experience of psychoanalytical categories and determinants was played out quickly in the 1920s, by the Surrealists with their embrace of irrationality and dream, and by such authors as Hermann Hesse and Luigi Pirandello. The more dominant strain of realizing a perspective on individual consciousness occurs in directions that deviate from, and that also eventually deny, the psychoanalytic.

Samuel Beckett, like Joyce Irish-born but, unlike him, from a Protestant upbringing, published *Murphy* in 1938. Unlike the Joycean vision of the city, the nation, and history intertwined with the sensory world of daily experience and reified through the stream of associative consciousness, Beckett portrays a character who exists in utter and abject disassociation from his surroundings. He creates his own rhythm of being-in-the-world, strapping himself to a rocking chair and gyrating himself into a state of self-possession. Murphy's intentions are stripped bare; he embraces nonbeing and nonexistence. This is a consciousness absorbed in self and devoured exclusively by mental and emotional autonomy. All that is external to the individual recedes. The acceleration of the recession is obvious, and is carried on in many instances, not the least of them in Beckett's later prose, *Watt* (1953), *Molloy* (1951), *Malone Dies* (1952), *The Unnamable* (1953), and *Waiting for Godot* (1954), a drama.

Contemporary to *Murphy* was the publication of Jean-Paul Sartre's *Nausea*. Its protagonist, Roquentin, is a historian who has sought refuge in the coastal city of Bouville (Mud Town). His alienation is not only from his vocation, for he drops all concern for the past, but from himself as well. When he looks at his own hands he recognizes that they are, as he is, but an extension of the external material world, which is by its nature a source of alienation. He is confronted with his own feeling of nonbeing. Both Murphy and Roquentin start from acceptance of the proposition that God is dead. This is no matter of contention or debate for either: it is an assumption that has become a given, unworthy of further inquiry. It is the central given of what it now must mean to be starting over again, from scratch, to make a life into a destiny from the starting point of nothingness.

Several movies, as well, in France in the late 1930s witnessed the combining of theme and character into what appears at first glance to be a more simple and straightforward narrative portrayal of a pessimistic fatalism. In Julien Duvivier's *Pépé-le-Moko* and two films by Marcel Carné, *Quai des Brumes* (1938) and *Daybreak Comes* (1939), the protagonists are confronted with the limitation of human possibilities, and the essential qualities of situations from which there is no exit. The Duvivier and Carné films are far more conventional in their narratives than either *Murphy* or *Nausea*. The narrative conventions and demands of the motion picture had not yet, even in the hands of these able directors, been manipulated successfully enough to go beyond the problems of overcoming limitations imposed by dint of the plastic materials of film itself. The dilemma of the richness of the world and of being-in-the-world that is contained in the moving image itself was at the core of this problem. Yet insofar as the plastic materials and the limitations of the medium would permit, *Pépé-le-Moko*, *Quai des Brumes*, and *Daybreak Comes* explored the confrontation with the emptiness of the world and the nothingness of self.

Further discussion of this shift in individual consciousness cannot be sustained without reference to the term "existentialism." Perhaps this is unfortunate; it may be that introducing the term at this point will result in more confusion than clarity. The purpose of doing so, however, is to deal fleetingly with a complicated and frequently misunderstood phenomenon. Existentialism is not a philosophy, but rather a point of view. It lacks system and, in fact, is intended precisely to avoid subjection to analysis as necessitated by formulation of a system. It posits that there is no given "human nature," a position most succinctly expressed in the Sartrean slogan, "Existence precedes essence." It departs from the categories of a determinant psychology in which prior experiences, repressed in the unconscious, both limit and channel the options of response subsequently available to the individual in situations to which they are linkd: hence, the existentialist critique of Freud in favor of an open-ended emphasizing of the necessity to choose. This implies a certain kind of freedom of will (a problematic phrase to use because of its patently religious connotations, especially in Catholic doctrine) that may be called radical, nontranscendent, and nondeterministic. From this perspective the individual's freedom and responsibility to choose is bounded neither by God, nor by the imprint of social environment, nor by the psychological residue left from prior experience. This might be called a version of "free will" without God, without repentance, and without the hope of salvation. Hence it might be considered a nearly unbearable burden upon the individual, were it not also devoid of a sense of sin, either original or commissional.

In the existential turn of mind the question "Why is there anything at all rather than nothing?" is a significant point of departure for reflecting on the nature of human consciousness. Morally, this ends in a feeling of guilt even though the world is meaningless. Culturally, this starting point has translated into a perception of the absurdity not only of the material social context in which we live, but of the situation itself that is essential to the human condition.

Receptivity to the existential point of view appears to be a matter more of temperament than of intellect. That observation reflects the difference—not just in degree, but in kind—between existentialism and all past philosophy, as we have understood that term in the Western world. To those who are insensitive to the existential temperament, the enactments in representational works that may be labeled "existential" are perplexing and disturbing. To such readers these works often seem geared to the portrayal of human situations that are morose, hopeless, and perversely irredeemable. However, the notion that such works are nihilistic is naive. On the contrary, they are a response to the accelerated drift toward nihilism that Nietzsche feared in the late nineteenth century. They are a reaction against that sweep toward the abyss of nihilism that had been borne witness to across the breadth of Western Europe since the First World War. Undoubtedly, certain works in the existential vein wander close to the brink of the nihilistic abyss. Their purpose, however, is not to breach it.

In retrospect, it appears that the brief triumph of science, positivism, and optimistic rationalism in the decades immediately prior to the First World War held back the drift toward nihilism. Disillusionment with and suspicion of these buffers was present in certain quarters, but not yet widespread. For all practical purposes the course of war from 1914 to 1918 marked an abrupt end for those buffering elements of confidence and quiescence. That breakdown registered widely and soon found its parallel in nearly every facet of life and experience in Western Europe.

That particular aspect of individual consciousness which, for convenience, is labeled "existential" found precedence in isolated examples from the time prior to World War I, but was nurtured only from the 1920s and called into being in its own right only by the mid-1930s. Such an attempt at dating this sort of a phenomenon is always problematic; we must be satisfied, however, that in this instance the sketchy profile suffices. The existential perspective on individual consciousness became serious, widespread, and for a time nearly definitive of individual consciousness in Western Europe only right after 1945.

Often it is believed that the existential point of view arose directly out of the French Resistance to the German Occupation of 1940–1944. The connecting links are tenuous, yet an interpretation made on the basis of them is not implausible. It is misleading, however, in any instance in which the notion of causation is overemphasized. The tracings that resulted in the existential perspective being launched with a vengeance in Europe right after World War II had a long prehistory. The experiences of the Occupation (and of the Resistance to it) were significant in crystallizing those tracings into a relatively unified worldview. To paraphrase Jean-Paul Sartre, the situation after the fall of France in June 1940 condensed the issue of freedom and individual authenticity. During the German Occupation those living under it were denied liberty and freedom, as we normally understand those concepts. Yet, as Sartre points out, never were certain individuals, who in consciousness could grasp what the genuine situation was, more free than at that very time. The Occupation meant that a gesture frowned upon by the Germans, a word overheard by an agent, or a meeting on the street might lead to arrest, detainment and interrogation, imprisonment, or death. It is in just such a situation that the individual becomes aware of the consequence of every gesture and word. Such a situation effectively brackets out the normal and conventional assumptions by which we distinguish and label only certain actions as being of genuine import and consequence.

The existential perspective on individual consciousness proceeds from recognition of the necessity to take responsibility for oneself in a radical posture of authenticity. Put simply, this means accepting the responsibility of being in the world and recognizing that all choices are significant. Thus there is no legitimate recourse to the posture of claiming to choose not to choose.

This line of thinking dates, at least, to the late eighteenth century. The slogan, "One cannot choose not to choose," can be found in Hegel's *Encyclopedia*, and the notion itself may be regarded as clarifying Immanuel Kant's "categorical imperative." Through the nineteenth century, however, the social demands and political consequences of the age did not warrant the individual embracing the vital and potent necessity of choice and commitment.

For Western humankind, the stakes rose dramatically with the course of the First World War and its immediate aftermath. The assumptions of an entire civilization had been challenged. The stakes were raised again, and the second time with a quantum leap, when the human prospect was assessed at the hour zero of May 1945. Then, as astute an observer as André Malraux suggested that the possibility confronting Western civilization was that the death of God would be followed by the "Death of Man." Since 1945, in that awareness, many European intellectuals have chosen distinctive paths of response to that dilemma.

One path, represented by Sartre, is the choice of political engagement and commitment. The other, represented by Albert Camus, is the embracing of emptiness and negation as wholeheartedly as possible in the hope of a working through and beyond them. After the Holocaust and after Hiroshima little space is left for escape. The intertwined links of culpability—the crimes of both commission and omission—served to close what exits had remained open.

The individual whose situation is rooted in estrangement and detachment has been portrayed repeatedly in prose, in drama, and in the cinema since the Second World War. The standard figure in this form of expression, the nearly classic anti-hero, is Mersault, the protagonist of *The Stranger* by Camus (1940). The novel begins with the sparse, haunting line: "Mother died yesterday, or perhaps it was today. I really don't remember." His tone of detachment, his lack of socialization, is carried forth from these lines. There is a mechanical and quasiphotographic quality in Merseault's observations of the world around him. This is not the photographic quality of the individual sensitized in the self-conscious mode of Christopher Isherwood's "I am a camera" approach to his Berlin stories from the early 1930s. It is a consciousness itself that reacts like a mechanism, recording only the surface observations of a world that offers too much to the human senses (at the same time framing what it offers in conventions) to be grasped and made intelligible. Merseault is not devoid of either sensitivity or sympathy. He shows this in his attitude toward the elderly fellow boarder in the residence where he lives, who keeps an old, mangy dog. In that relationship there is a suggestion of the love-hate, the sympathy-abuse, and the tortured symbiosis that intertwines lives inextricably, without reason though sometimes with rhyme. Merseault is almost a sleepwalker. His motivation and his passion are obscure. When he shoots a young Algerian on the beach, he seems only caught in the light of the sun that fills the sky and the heat of midafternoon. His finger pulls the trigger in a manner that can be described only as detached, unmotivated, and uprooted. In prison, awaiting trial, Merseault is visited by a priest. Only in this encounter can he respond with anger and feeling, not in consciousness of what he believes but rather in spontaneous awareness of what it is that he rejects.

The representation of the detached and solitary figure, the individual not socialized into convention, the anti-hero of alienated perspective, has become central to the elaboration of individual consciousness in Western European works of affecting presence. Take, for example, the 1970 novel by the Austrian-born Peter Handke. Handke's equivalent to Merseault is a construction worker named Joseph Bloch, formerly a soccer goaltender. In the *Goalie's Anxiety at the Penalty Kick* Bloch is dismissed from his job, wanders about the city, picks up a young woman, and strangles her. Her name is Gerda, a fact Bloch did not really want to know. He simply became the victim of her blurting it out. They are in her apartment together, she playing Italian pop songs on the phonograph.

> But then everything seemed to irritate him more and more. He wanted to answer her but broke off in mid-sentence because he assumed that she already knew what he had to say. She grew restless and started moving about the room; she was looking for something to do, smiling stupidly now and then. They passed the time by turning records over and changing them. She got up and lay down on the bed; he sat down next to her. Was he going to work today? she wanted to know.
> Suddenly he was choking her. From the start his grip was so tight that she'd never had a chance to think he was kidding. Bloch heard voices outside in the hall. He was scared to death. He noticed some stuff running out of her nose. She was gurgling. Finally he heard a snapping noise. It sounded like a stone on a dirt road slamming against the bottom of a car. Saliva had dripped onto the linoleum. [Peter Handke, *Goalie's Anxiety at the Penalty Kick*, 1972, trans. Michael Roloff]

Bloch leaves and goes to a border village where he takes lodging at an inn. He watches this new world into which he has placed himself. One day he finds himself standing on the sidelines at a soccer match with a salesman. The salesman recollects the time he saw a player break his leg, and the cracking sound of it could be heard to the highest rows in the stadium. Bloch comments on the goaltender. A penalty kick is called. It is shot directly into the goalie's hands.

The Stranger is closed and resolved: Merseault is convicted and condemned to death, more for the cold-heartedness he displayed at his mother's funeral than for the murder of the Algerian (for which there were extenuating circumstances). *The Goalie's Anxiety* is open-ended; in it there is no shift in awareness akin to the shift that occurred with Merseault in his reaction against the priest's visit to him.

In the enactment in writing the reader experiences still the consciousness of the individual who verbalizes, even in the flattened tones of a Merseault or a Bloch. In the motion picture, such verbalization, such flattening out of the narration, is not necessary. Silence itself can be depicted directly. Distancing can be seen rather than described. In *Eclipse*, Michelangelo Antonioni's movie of 1962, Monica Vitti portrays a young woman who dabbles in translation work for income and who strolls through life from the comfortable, yet sterile and seemingly inconsequential, environment of her new apartment in a suburb of Rome. Her financial situation seems adequate; her surroundings reflect the trappings of what might be called voguishly liberated independence. Yet her life's experience is extraordinarily slim, as conveyed by its surroundings as well as by her tentative, unmotivated, and thwarted relationships to others. She neither manifests nor expresses the pathos of self-pity or the passion of anger; beneath the surface she simply lives both. Her encounter with society—that is, her visit to the frenzied stock exchange where her mother plays the market daily—is an encounter with the energized, the irrational, that which is apparently out of control. There are long periods of silence in *Eclipse*, beginning with the opening sequence in which she and her lover Giorgio come to a parting. Visually, the film is punctuated by various spatial splits. Aurally, it is rife with passages of silence, which are direct, prolonged, and disturbing. *Eclipse* ends with a sequence of five to six minutes of shots of an intersection and its environs near her apartment. The loneliness, the vacuity, and the solitariness of a world of objects are depicted—a barrel slowly draining rainwater, a construction site where no work is being done, the arriving and departing of a city bus, a nurse wheeling a child's pram.

If the novelist Gustave Flaubert's character Emma Bovary symbolized the situation of many European women at mid-nineteenth century, Antonioni's protagonist in *Eclipse* represents the frustrations of many contemporary women who may be comfortable financially, yet feel isolated and estranged. In Emma Bovary's disquietude and tentative rebellion against the ennui of bourgeois provincial life is a sensibility yearning for the romanticized excitement and allure of something more. The protagonist's life in *Eclipse* is fraught with anxiety, surrounded by sterility, turning ever back in upon itself—yet in that turning she discovers nothingness.

Of the established conventions of representational fiction developed in the nineteenth century, two divergent genres were especially important in the exploration of aspects of individual consciousness. They were the *Bildungsroman* (or "novel of coming of age") and the detective novel. Twentieth-century narrative fiction in Western Europe, both written and filmed, has continued to the present both themes, although their purity has been compromised many times over, and their psychological and social returns continue to diminish. The central contention of each, which was rooted in a particular point of view, and which found as a point of reference a relatively specific ideological orientation, has been abandoned—indeed, even self-consciously negated. This is true especially since the end of the Second World War.

Increasingly, the aspects of individual consciousness have become permeated with the sensibilities of stasis, of a continuum that cuts across feeling, of no exit. A novel of education must accept as a point of departure the notion of change, of transformation and catharsis, won perhaps at the cost of great inner struggle against those outside forces of depersonalization, arbitrary constraint, and the pressures of conventionality. This theme has of course continued with a certain updating, in novels such as Günter Grass's *Cat and Mouse* (1961) and *The Tin Drum* (1959), Alan Sillitoe's *Saturday Night and Sunday Morning* (1958) and *The Loneliness of the Long Distance Runner* (1959), and Georgio Bassanni's *Behind the Door* (1964), in Ermanno Olmi's film *The Sound of Trumpets* (1958), and in Peter Schaffer's drama *Equus* (1973). The sense in them of overcoming the confrontational circumstances of being individual and being oneself is tortured and convoluted. The struggle of the protagonists is not heroic, but displaced into an alternative consciousness of humanity winning out only by a certain idiosyncratic willingness to drop the struggle, to give in; not to triumph in an act of will but to deceive and avoid successfully.

Hence, individual consciousness has come to be rooted in recognition of negation. It is not the world's hostility but simply its indifference that thwarts the individual. In this perception of the human condition in which rebellion is not against the visible, but rather against the invisible—that which is already part of the self rather than extraneous to it and in competition with it—a new consciousness is enacted.

It is perhaps this indifference, this dehumanization, this strangely undramatic possible death of man that underscores too the line of fascination with the act of crime against man. When the detective novel of the late nineteenth century reached its apogee in England, it could be interpreted as reflecting in narrative fiction the triumph of rationalistic and liberal faith in individual acuity, capacity for ordering of the universe, and personal domination over evil (not as a ubiquitous human condition but in its social ramification as criminality) and deception. However, since the early-nineteenth-century Romantics, and continuing to the present, the criminal act has been a point of departure for exploring the aspects of individual consciousness, reality, and illusion. In addition to *The Stranger* and *The Goalie's Anxiety*, other well-known examples are Jean Genet's *Deathwatch* (1942), Harold Pinter's *The Dumbwaiter* (1956), Jean-Luc Godard's 1959 film *Breathless*, and nearly all the plays and novellas of Friedrich Dürrenmatt. In Alain Robbe-Grillet's movie *Trans-Europe Express* (1966), in Antonioni's *Blow-Up*, made in Great Britain in 1968, and in the Joseph Losey–Harold Pinter film *The Accident* (1967), the theme of the criminal act—of its being or nonbeing, of its veracity or lack of it, of the open-endedness of guilt—is played out. Here is the displacement of the interest in fiction from a criminal act as a point of departure for the amazing exploits of the rational individual who unravels the complexity into meaning; that is, into solution. Rather, the criminal act is an act of disassociated willfulness, a lonely shout in the universe, a source of last-ditch excitement for the world-weary, or a remaining field in which virtuosity—so often denied in corporate and mass society—is still possible.

Increasingly in the twentieth century, an open society has replaced social order; opportunity has replaced privilege; man has replaced God, taken God into himself, ended the delusion of projection and turned it into the self-perpetuating illusion of absorption; in turn, things have replaced man himself, the material universe ostensibly offering its own redemption of itself. Without the rigidity of structure—i.e., the standardized and conventional modes of ordering experience—not only has the experiential become an open field but the veracity, and even the possibility, of authentic experience has become subject to question. The perception of uprootedness, homelessness, and alienation has become a psychic condition, related to social reality only in that that reality offers no longer a clear connecting link to what is going on inside.

The turning inward, and then radically outward, but going beyond the natural surfaces and contours of the experiential world, has been pioneered, chronologically, in Western European painting. Parallel to Kurtz's discovery of a world of spirit and inner power that overwhelms his rational individualistic defenses in Africa, was the cubists' discovery (their work had appeared within a few years of the publication of *Heart of Darkness*), from African woodcarving, of ways of reducing the external appearances of the surface world of experience to their geometrical equivalents. Since cubism, painting in the Western world has led a zigzag course toward abstraction and analytical constructs, toward hard edges and design, and away from representationalism altogether. Abstractionism itself has tended to become increasingly devoid of referents to the experienced material world, or to the inner world perceived in the mind's eye projected expressionistically. This sort of art frequently exists strictly as decoration, totally unrepresentational and devoid of mimetic connectedness either to the experienced or to that which is perceived residue of experience processed internally.

In its quest beyond naturalism, twentieth-century representational writing—and then, after 1945, cinematography—have shown signs of pushing toward greater abstractness, greater concern with rhythm, pattern, and sensibility. In so doing a vision of individual consciousness has been posited that embraces the void, and that explores the individual's situation and crisis-in-anxiety as one of isolation and alienation. Notably, however, that perception of isolation and alienation inclines away from seeing this dilemma as a consequence of the hostile pressures of external social reality.

Chapter Three
Revolutionary Consciousness

D URING THE TWENTIETH-CENTURY the locale of revolution has been first Russia, and then various places in Asia, Africa, the Middle East, and Latin America. This represented a decided shift. In the nineteenth century, revolutionary episodes took place almost exclusively in the European heartland. Between the uprisings of 1830 and the gallant exploits of the Paris Commune in 1870-1871, revolution had raged, in 1848, if briefly, across the European continent. From Paris to Budapest, and from Sicily to Prussia, revolutions—either on behalf of national liberation, or of national unification, or for political and social reforms—engulfed the continent. Only the geographic extremities of Europe were spared: the British Isles, Spain, Russia, and Scandinavia.

In spite of these traditions as well as the fact that the emotional ethos of revolutionary consciousness was native to the European heartland, Europe proper (excluding Russia) has witnessed few revolutionary episodes since 1871. In 1918-1919 there were revolutions in both Germany and Hungary which were brief and had no long-term significance. Since the Second World War only the short-lived uprising of May-June 1968 in France appears to have been a genuine revolution-in-the-making.

In a simple way, it has been the Bolshevik seizure of power in Russia late in 1917, and the party's eventual triumph in the civil war that followed, that altered the parameters of revolutionary consciousness in Western Europe. Subsequently, that alteration was to prove both fraught with inspiration and burdened with liability. For leftist thinkers the very fact of a revolution in "backwards" Russia was itself perplexing. Orthodox Marxism, of course, had anticipated that the capitalist system would self-destruct and the radicalized proletariat seize power where industrial capitalism was most highly developed—in Germany, for example. The happy circumstance of revolution in a society that was ostensibly not yet ready for it led to decades of academic debate over how this had occurred. That debate itself has yielded little that accounts any better for the revolution's success in Russia than the observations of the Bolshevik leader himself, Vladimir Ilyich Lenin. He theorized that tsarist Russia was vulnerable to revolution because it was, in fact, the "weakest link" in the chain of industrialized capitalist nations. Worldwide, revolution in the twentieth century has been in underdeveloped and nonindustrial societies. Still, in academic circles especially in Western Europe, the debate over the Russian paradox continues even today.

The concern here is not with the nuances or subtleties, or even with the fact, of this debate. It is, rather, with the way in which the Bolshevik triumph entered into and colored revolutionary consciousness in Western Europe. This coloration was not complete until the burst of revolutionary activity that marked the end of the First World War (1918-1919) had dissolved in failure. This failure underscored the dashed hopes of those who expected a spreading paroxysm of revolution to engulf and devour the established regimes on the Continent. The failure came at a time precisely when the internal contradictions in the established bourgeois system appeared to be more evident than ever after the four years of attrition, dislocation, and destructiveness of the war itself. The second element that added to the coloration was the later triumph of Stalinism in the Soviet Union. By 1927, with Stalin's announcement of the First Five-Year Plan to force the Soviet Union's industrialization, the seeds were sown for a long, drawn-out crisis of conscience for the Western European Left. Moreover, Stalinism meant the clear and unabashed harnessing of communist ideology and internationalism to Soviet foreign policy, which itself turned out to be only an extension of traditional, prerevolutionary Russian foreign policy. The crisis of conscience was heightened with the rise and triumph of fascism in Italy and of national socialism in Germany during the years between the First and the Second World Wars. Combined, these developments proved perplexing to forward-looking individuals and parties in Western Europe. The call to antifascism led many of them to stick with the Soviet Union at all costs—until the mid-1950s, when the Soviet repression of the Hungarian revolt finally fractured orthodox leftism in Western Europe. Since the mid-1950s the fracture in orthodox leftism has developed in at least four directions: (1) the emergence of the New Left; (2) the establishment of a conventionalized neo-Marxism, now at the core of much of Western European thought;

(3) the definition of a Eurocommunism relatively free of Moscow's bidding; and (4) the rise of random terrorism, especially in the 1970s. This melange contains elements of neo-Marxism that have extended into various academic exercises, forms of anarchism, sympathy for the Third World, hostility toward both superpowers (especially the United States), generational tensions, and alternative parties like the West German "Greens."

The central irony of revolutionary consciousness in the Western European heartland is, however, that while revolutionary consciousness is fractured on its native soil the mythos of revolution has become one of Western civilization's most successful export commodities. The idea of the rightness of recourse to force in redress of injustice—political, economic, or social—that today flourishes everywhere in the world originated, in its modern version, in Western Europe. Eighteenth-century Western thought hardly discovered the notion of rebellion, of course. However, the *philosophes* of the French Enlightenment spelled out the idea that progress goes along with—and, in fact, may depend upon—revolution.

Insofar as most revolutionary movements and factions in the world today acknowledge links with some form of Marxism or Marxist revisionism, the influence on them of Western thought and mythos becomes clearer. Marx, an intellectual child of the Enlightenement, championed its rationalist mentality as well as the scientism that was on the rise in Europe in his own lifetime. The central message of radical equality in all aspects of social and economic life was manifest already during the course of the revolution in France. Gracchus Babeuf, who was guillotined for his political activities in 1797, and his followers in the Society of Equals were calling for a rudimentary communism. They recognized that political reforms (e.g., the right to vote, representative institutions, and justice under the law) were insufficient to guarantee liberty and fraternity in society. Hence, they called for authentic economic eqality as a basis for human liberation.

Karl Marx eventually broke with the Utopian Socialists. He rejected their reformism, wishful thinking, and romantic nostalgia in favor of what he came to call scientific socialism. Although the early writings (pre-1848) of Marx indicate that his humanistic orientation and certain of his concerns were rooted in a brand of romanticism, his mature thought (post-1848) was materialist. Marx's emphasis became deterministic, accompanied by relatively concrete predictions of the deepening and intensifying of the modern class struggles between bourgeoisie and proletariat and by confidence in the inevitability of revolution. Marx's political economy came to rest in the certitude that control of the means of production and of wealth would become more concentrated in fewer hands, and the ranks of the bourgeoisie would diminish. Concurrently the proletariat would grow in numbers and its situation would become more marginal, bordering increasingly on material disaster. This notion of the progressive deterioration of the economic status of the proletariat and its ever-increasing deprivation, together with its progression in numbers and strength, is a strong component of the Marxist legacy.

Revolutionary consciousness in modern, Western industrial societies accommodates both the informative value of Marx's analysis of the historical situation and his predictions, and their liabilities as well. The apparent inaccuracy of a number of Marx's predictions remains a target for opponents and critics. These predictions have proven to be a source of difficulty for adherents, yet also a point of departure for some of the most clever and subtle argumentation in modern Western thought.

For example, since a major dilemma for the Left lies in Marx's prediction of deterioration of the material circumstances of the proletariat even as their numbers grow, elaborate arguments have been advanced to explain why this has not come about. One of these (and perhaps the best-established among them) is that the capitalist industrial societies have succeeded in "exporting" the inherent burdens of the economic system beyond their own national boundaries. This argument originated from observation of the imperialist scramble at the end of the nineteenth century and reached its definitive expression at the time of the First World War. Early proponents of this view include the Russian revolutionary thinker and leader V. I. Lenin and the British economist J. A. Hobson. According to them and others, the controlling and dominant class in modern capitalist industrial states has deftly transferred the economic burdens of the system from its own proletariat population to the exploited inhabitants of the underdeveloped regions of the world. In simple terms this emphasizes the notion of imperialism as an advanced stage of modern capitalism. It also provides an explanation of how industrial capitalism has created a situation in which domestic working-class income, and even economic and social mobility, can be preserved at acceptable levels. These aspects of the advanced capitalist system are preserved at the cost of the ever-more extensively exploited peoples of the nonindustrial world.

A more pedestrian argument is that the capitalists, through their political operatives, have learned to disguise the inherent deprivations and injustice of the economic system over which they preside through stop-gap palliative measures. Within this deceptive cooptation, social reform, welfarism, and a variety of short-term and redistributive measures cover up the limitations of an irrational system. However, they relieve only superficial symptoms of exploitation rather than tending to eradicate the causes of exploitation. The bourgeois states succeed in this dirty work by fostering a false sense of security in an uncontrollable economy, and by perpetuating legislatively the liberal-democratic myth of equality of opportunity.

A relatively recent elaboration on the critique of capitalism is in a more personal and psychological category. The argument runs that contemporary capitalist bourgeois societies permit and even endorse all sorts of counter culture and quasi-rebellious life-styles, not only giving them sanction but also exploiting their allures as yet other branches of consumerism. This form of cooptation is manipulated in order to discharge the available collective energy for authentic revolutionary action in the direction of random escapism and narcissistic hedonism. Central to it are the electronic media, the proliferation of a drug subculture, the breakdown in sexual mores and prohibitons, the allure of fashion, decoration, and accouterment (i.e., radical chic), and so forth.

Within this intellectual environment have taken place the enactments in narrrative prose, dramatic writing, and motion pictures that posit a modern and contemporary revolutionary consciousness. One aspect of this consciousness, not unique to the twentieth century but surely elaborated with particular intensity during it, is the notion of the work of art as an act of social engagement, political commitment, or partisan propagation of specific ideas.

In the twentieth century the proliferation of forms of expression and communication (such as movies and television), the spread of literacy, and the growth of reproduction technologies (film, recording, photocopier) mean that the work of art can now reach larger audiences. Access to the work itself is no longer necessarily limited by one's location, economic status, or educational background. Art forms have become more numerous and democratized, and traditional cultural elites have surrendered much of their control over them.

A combination of technological, socioeconomic, and cultural developments heighten the possibility that the work of art may edify and propagandize large numbers of people. This renders all the more difficult the problem as to what sort of art is appropriate to manifest revolutionary consciousness. Even in the nineteenth century, the matter was hardly simple. Marx and his collaborator, Friedrich Engels, had little to say on the matter, except to praise several specific novels and to urge that radical intent may be unnecessary to the effective literary work. Generally, classical Marxist thought argues that culture, thought, and works of art are reflections of the material conditions and class antagonisms that obtain in a society. It follows that the dominant art forms will express interests of the dominant class, as perceived by that class!

The writer or filmmaker then is confronted with this central question: to what extent is it efficacious to attempt to subvert the dominant forms, which are the representational forms, to the expression of revolutionary consciousness? If one decides to use a dominant form of expression for revolutionary edification, a secondary question is just what one should create? Naturalistic works may contribute to lucidity about the class situation. Socialist realist works may manifest the consciousness of collective identification, action, and heroism, or the idea of surrendering the ego to the historical progress of the masses. Artistic work that is multidimensional, abstract, distorted from surface reality, and unbounded or "shoreless" may be considered revolutionary, too. The debate over what is correct revolutionary art is heated.

One of the characteristics of bourgeois art is that it is art by the bourgeois and for it, but frequently in opposition to it. Its exploratory and critical nature is aimed often at the consumer, just as the bourgeois mentality is commonly self-critical. This notable tendency to self-criticism seems to derive from a collective psychology of insecurity, instability, and identity and role crisis; which in turn derives from the unwillingness and/or inability of the bourgeoise, *as a class*, to accept its dominance in modern society.

The renegade bourgeois, who revolts against his or her own class, faces another paradox. If one takes seriously the Marxist claim of the historical inevitability of the proletariat revolution, the role of the bourgeois sympathizer in this process is dubious. Culturally, the primary answer has been for the renegade bourgeois to identify with the avant-garde. The term itself means simply "vanguard," and its original usage was political. In 1878 the anarchist Mikhail Bakunin founded a journal of politics and protest called *L'Avant-Garde*. The journal itself was soon defunct. The term was shifted, with the rise of the notion of "art for art's sake" at the very end of the nineteenth century, to the sphere of artistic culture. Here it found a home, referring to those ahead of their times who are leading the way to what will one day be commonly accepted forms of expression. This implies setting off one's work, and also one's life-style, from the established norms of convention and taste. Both self-conscious and self-promoting, the avant-garde sees itself as an "advance front" leading the change in consciousness.

Since the 1960s the phenomenon of counterculture groups has become widespread in the Western industrial societies. The "happening" of the 1960s was a throwback to the conduct of the Parisian avant-garde in the years before the First World War. The penchant for performance in the 1960s—shocking to bourgeois propriety— dates back to dadaism and surrealism. Confronting the "establishment" with an assault upon its values dates from the earliest years of this century. In this context one of those values is art itself: one of the main modes through which those values are felt to be expressed is that object of affecting presence that is called the work of art. Prior to the First World War, the futurists declared themselves proponents of an aesthetic of speed, seeking to break old syntax, rhythm, and harmony, recognizing the beauty of the rapid-fire machine-gun. The dadists, who emerged in midcourse of the war itself, proclaimed themselves artists against art, ready to put the liberating act of destruction on an equal plane with the act of creativity.

That dadaist emergence occurred in Zurich, Switzerland, right across the street from where Lenin and his Bolshevik cohorts were working out a revised revolutionary theory. In their negation of traditional and established assumptions, the dadists paralleled several predecessors. These included Nietzsche's critique of past philosophy; Planck's and Einstein's assaults upon classical physics; the various philosophers who questioned the adequacy of language to express authentic meaning and value; the embrace of primitivism in the painting of the cubists and of the fauvists.

All these challenges to established notions, ideas, conventions, and traditions came after 1870, and they accelerated after 1900. After the collapse of the relatively spontaneous and broad-based revolt of the commune in Paris in the aftermath of France's debacle in the Franco-Prussian war, the political Left in Europe paled. The call to the barricades in the Parisian working-class district of Montmartre marked a brief revival of the empassioned ethos of revolution that had perished on the barricades in that same city in 1848. After its defeat, the Left throughout Europe shifted gears. One shift in the reappraisal of tactics and programs, was in the direction of moderation. Those Social Democrats in Germany who led this revisionism had, by the mid-1890s, emerged in the majority of their party. Germany's proletariat, possibly the most viable revolutionary force in Europe, had opted for moderation and reform. Cooptation had been running apace since the late 1870s in Germany in any case, spurred by the social reforms undertaken under the aegis of the conservative Otto von Bismarck.

All across Europe in the years after 1871, nationalism displaced domestic social aggression successfully into national patriotism, often ending in a demand for imperialistic aggrandizement. Immigration—primarily to the United States—eased certain economic and social crises in a number of spots. Only marginally, and even somewhat higher up on the socioeconomic ladder, did imperialism itself provide much of a release for economic and social malaise. The rampant imperialism of the late nineteenth century was primarily an imperialism of economic management, not of colonizing and resettlement.

Beyond both Social-Democratic revisionism and leftist academicism, which tended to grind revolutionary zeal into convoluted theory, were the anarchist bomb throwers, seemingly intent on blasting society literally into the classless, stateless millenium that Marx had promised. The impetus and impulse to violent means passed to various anarchist groups, whose numbers grew at a rate roughly equal to the growth of their political unreliability and instability. Their intent was revolutionary, of course, but patently not systematically so, and surely on a basis difficult to align with materialist determinism and dialectical analyses of the historic situation. Between anarchism and revisionism the Left lost much ground in the fight to assert the cultural primacy of revolutionary consciousness.

After 1871 trade unionism grew, making greater inroads some places than others. The bourgeoisie felt threatened by the trade-union movement; on the other hand, acquiescence to union activities within certain parameters made it less likely that laborers would seek redress of grievances through more direct and revolutionary political organizations. Among the many seductions and diversions for the energies of the masses was anti-Semitism, a phenomenon whose presence grew and whose nature changed quite perceptibly toward the end of the nineteenth century and at the beginning of the twentieth. The political exploitation of the Jew-as-scapegoat became a special kind of wrinkle for modern European politics after 1870. European anti-Semitism was nothing new, of course. However, its complexity and subtlety, its economic and political and collective psychological dimensions, and its daily presence, became much greater than ever before. In one direction, anti-Semitism was linked with purportedly "scientific" ideas pointing to the biological or racial nature of "Jewishness" over and beyond its actual religious and cultural characteristics. Used in this way, anti-Semitism was exploitable as a diversion of attention and energy away from real grievances and sources of economic and social injustice toward imagined ones rooted in racial antagonism. It was exploited politically almost all across Europe in the decade prior to the First World War, with marked differences in responsiveness here and there, sporadically. It was another element displacing the resentment and inner social tension, in this case toward the shadow ever-present on the European landscape—the Jew!

The Left engaged in debates over revolutionary or reformist strategy, and attempts at internationalism in the years immediately preceding the First World War. But in August 1914, when the chips were down, leftist parties and trade-union groups almost universally rushed to take nationalist positions. The political representatives of the Left voted for war credits in parliaments where they sat, the proletariat evinced as much war enthusiasm and blood lust as any element in society, trade unions committed their collective shoulders to the wheel of the war machine, and international solidarity withered on the vine. The Left proved to be extraordinarily loyal to the myths of the ruling elites and to the conflict waged on behalf of the material interests of those elites.

Beneath this temporary collapse of the Left, internationalism, and proletariat solidarity, lay the makings of a very different future. As the war sank into a bloody stalemate in 1916, with the end nowhere in sight, more radical and independent elements in leftist parties began to criticize their own governments. Splinter groups formed that in several instances would become communist parties right after the war. Most importantly, in Russia the two-stage revolt in 1917 against the tsarist regime ended with the Bolsheviks' ascendancy there by year's end. Lenin and the Bolsheviks had the initial advantage that they were not committed to continuing the war effort, as were the more moderate and centrist elements, which had attempted to fill the power vacuum in Russia after the first, February, rebellion against the tsarist regime. In simple language, the seemingly endless and unwinnable war of attrition that the First World War had become was itself the issue on which revolution in Russia hinged, and toward which the bolshevik policy of unilateral withdrawal from the conflict provided the measure of advantage in its successful grab for power. Other nations witnessed mutiny in the army (France in 1917) or navy (Kiel, Germany, in October 1918). Unprepared civilian revolution broke out in Munich just a few days before the armistice. At war's end, rebellion seemed on the agenda—nearly everywhere in Central and Eastern Europe, at least. For there, with the end of both the German and the Austro-Hungarian empires, it appeared that only the leftist parties would be sufficiently disassociated from the defeated and discredited regimes to assume power.

The specter of revolution haunted not only the lands of the defeated governments: in France, England, and Italy the Left was radicalized after 1918. However, its effectiveness was blunted by the split in the Old International caused by the Bolshevik seizure of power. The postwar "red scare" reached as far as the United States, where the panic seemed grossly out of proportion to the threat. To a great many of those who shared the fear, no matter where they might be, the possibility registered that the Bolsheviks' seizure of power in Russia might spark a revolutionary conflagration engulfing the industrial nations. The Bolsheviks themselves seemed convinced at the time that the moment of global revolution was at hand. Lenin articulated his "21 points," which spelled the bright future of international revolution. Trotsky wagered his career on the premise that the Bolsheviks would promote worldwide revolt at any cost.

In Hungary proper a Communist regime was crushed. Across Germany government forces and right-wing volunteers suppressed the revolts by May 1919, but left a large Communist party for the Weimar Republic to contend with through the 1920s. In England, the Labour party grew (mainly at the expense of the waning Liberal party); it elected a prime minister in 1924, but showed every sign of moderating its posture as its party position improved. In France, by the end of 1920, a majority of the Socialist party had opted for radicalization by joining the Comintern and forming the French Communist Party (PCF).

In Italy, where the government in power waited out the revolutionary episodes and paralyzing strikes until they dissipated in 1920, the Socialists and the new Catholic Popular party grew in strength; most significant, however, was the antisocialist, anticommunist formulation that lay at the heart of the Fascist movement. Highly nationalistic, anticlerical, and presenting certain apparently radical demands, facism grew from fear of the Left and resentment that Italy did not enjoy the national glory she deserved.

The dislocations and disruptions in social, economic, and political life, the discrediting of established regimes and value systems, and the general disillusionment brought on by the First World War are surely the kinds of conditions most favorable to a growth of revolutionary fervor, leftist sentiment, and the appeal of radicalism in modern industrial states. It may be, however, that this triggers something quite complicated at the collective psychological level. The impetus to organized revolt against a modern or contemporary regime in an industrialized society may take as its point of departure injustices in the economic and social system. However, more important in determining the volatility of a situation may be a crisis of image, direction, and leadership, that is profound, thorough, and often linked with the nation's role and status in the world.

Although most general speculations are inappropriate, concerning the circumstances and conditions in a modernized society that are conducive to revolution, several observations obtain. First, no truly modernized society has ever experienced a successful revolution, and the only episodes approaching such a revolution have been in Germany (1918–1919) and France (1968). Second, a new form of revolutionary consciousness came into existence after the Bolsheviks seized power in Russia in October 1917. This event altered the entire range of feelings, ideas, perceptions, and levels of awareness of what revolution as a collective act means—or may mean. This presents a problem in surveying the past. The truly modern aspect of individual consciousness dates from the proclamation of the death of God in 1873; the truly modern aspect of Western revolutionary consciousness dates from the Bolshevik seizure of power in 1917. The one predates the other by nearly half a century. Yet both these specific occurrences have shaped the character of aspects of contemporary consciousness.

Even before Nietzsche announced the death of God, many may have doubted God, ignored God, or even denied God. Nonetheless, by that announcement, which itself eventually spread through Western thought and culture, the issue of the existence of God in relation to the human condition was altered. In similar fashion, many may have argued on behalf of Marx, wished for revolution, or courted it. After the Bolshevik seizure of power in Russia, however, the issue of revolution and revolutionary consciousness could never again be the same as it was before. It was when the implications of Nietzsche's announcement were becoming clear that modern individual consciousness began to take on a distinctive new shape (*circa* 1900). With the Bolshevik triumph there was no similar time lag. The transformed revolutionary ethos and consciousness was brought to expression in the heartland of Western Europe even before the Bolshevik hold on power in Russia was secure.

In 1919 Ernst Toller wrote a drama entitled *Mass Man*. The title itself denoted awareness that the "age of the masses," announced as commencing at various points from 1870 on, had arrived. So, as well, had the age of revolutionary anxiety and tortured conscience. Toller himself was an intellectual and military leader of the Bavarian Soviet Socialist Republic, and served in battle until the uprising finally was quelled in May 1919. A few years later he killed himself, apparently in a crisis over balancing his political commitment with his basic humanism.

The play takes up the compelling appeal of the idea of revolution, setting that appeal in the context of a conflict between the human being's social commitment and feelings of individuality. It does so through the dilemma of the protagonist, Sonia Irene L., juxtaposing the public sphere of responsiblity and action with the private sphere of reflection and sentiment. This dichotomy is common, so common in fact that it might be called characteristic of modern and contemporary mentality and sensibility. It is nearly definitive of the feeling that confronts many men and women. Hence, it can be taken as indicative of the discontinuity or the rupture that is sensed as being at the heart of the human condition in its distinctively modern (or contemporary) predicament. In *Mass Man* this thematic dualism is cast in counterpoint by the dramatic device of juxtaposing different sorts of staged sequences, primarily the naturalist with the dreamlike. There are elements of representation here that mesh with aspects considered "expressionist." The dream sequences serve to highlight the main character's problematic evolution toward revolutionary awareness: that is, toward acknowledging the necessity of violence.

The play is set in wartime; the First World War and its immediate aftermath are, after all, the backdrop to modern revolutionary consciousness and action. Thematically, this choice is telling: an established modern society becomes most vulnerable to revolution in the context of war's dislocations.

Sonia's call for a general strike is eclipsed by the beckoning of the "Nameless One," an allegorical figure representing the course of "history" and the anonymity of the "masses." Here is a juxtaposition that *Mass Man* does not ignore: the tension between the high-minded and detached desire for justice felt by Sonia, who might be said to represent the intellectual or middle-class rebel, and the willful, passionate, and destructive desire born of anger and envy that defines the revolutionary impetus of those in less enviable circumstances. Here there is a laying bare of the contradiction between revolutionary intention and revolutionary means, between individual will and collective forces, between tenderness and pity on the one hand and harshness and cynicism on the other. Sonia is, after all, the would-be "humanist" revolutionary. To the chant "The masses count," she replies, "Humanity counts."

Her naiveté is of the sort that makes her ripe for cooptation. Eventually, however, she comes to see the futility of a generous spirit that attains to little more than the shoddiness of bourgeois charity, as represented in *Mass Man* by the bankers' charity ball to aid the victims of a mining disaster: "A dance at the Stock Exchange . . . Against need . . . All proceeds to the poor." The established leftist critique of charity is here given its due. The givers are assuaging bad conscience, glossing over with their gifts all the causes of want. They are determining by their personal whim what is need and what is not, and, on top of all this, assuming a posture of righteousness about their sacrifices.

The capitalist may not be without some measure of compassion or of love; this perception is at the core of the tension Sonia feels about her husband, a well-to-do capitalist. There is a difference, however, between love of another individual and love of mankind. The basis of revolutionary consciousness is in the emotional progress toward love of mankind. That love, however, can be secured only by acts of violence against certain individuals on behalf of mankind.

To the bankers in the play, love is lust. They cannot conceive of love of mankind, love of humanity. This they declare to be unnatural, drawing upon either quasi-biological or quasi-psychological support for their position. Yet, the play does not simply explore descriptively the shortcomings of the dominant classes. Rather, it posits both that revolutionary violence is necessary and that it is outside the control of the revolutionaries, once initiated. "You murder for humanity just as the deluded ones killed for the state. Some of those truly thought that their country—their Fatherland—would redeem the world. Between the two I don't see any difference." Yet freedom can be won, and hence the love of humanity expressed, only through recourse to action and violence.

Mass Man points to the articulation of the complexity of revolutionary awareness and the direction in which it impels one. Notably, that direction is not a function of historical determinism. Rather it is an act of will attained to in full self-consciousness and at no small psychological expense. Written just after the First World War (and immediately subsequent to the rash of rebellion that followed the war's end), the play points to the issue of violence. For the First World War itself pointed to the exponential increase of violence and terror. The war produced enormous fissures in the facade of a civilization based upon rationality and the repression of aggressive impulses.

The war itself—in its duration, its scope, its ferocity, and its eventual dependency upon materials and technology—became a war of attrition. Everywhere Europeans had entered the war in 1914 with the baggage of a century of relative peace dragging behind them. Their model for warfare between major belligerent nation states was the Franco-Prussian clash of 1870–1871. It had been a brief, relatively clean, and professional war on the old scale, and civilians were scarcely subject to its violence. Unable to perceive the civil war in the United States (1861–1865) as the nineteenth-century pro-genitor of warfare in the twentieth century, Europeans in 1914 rushed to war. They were certain that warfare itself was still a matter of deftness, of strategy, and, moreover, a phenomenon still manageable in human terms and still understandable in such classic categories as heroism. The course of the war proved all these convictions to be naive. The proof was not absolutely conclusive, of course, for much of the old mentality and the old manners had not yet caught up with this new reality. That dissonance was, in itself, one of the genuine legacies of the war to end all wars, which marked the beginning of exponential and unending increase worldwide in the level of violence. A substantial aspect of the world we lost after World War I is that in the prior world, violence was more controlled, less all-encompassing, and justified in more discriminating frameworks. As Julien Benda, the French essayist, has suggested, for two thousand years men did evil but honored good. Only in the twentieth century is the recourse to violence justified intellectually rather than condemned.

It is always less problematic to think about revolution than to carry it out. Carrying it out involves not so much the challenges of the status-quo opposition as the dilemma of doing violence to humans on behalf of humanity. Distancing is always of help in such matters, as are situations in which the lines are drawn relatively clearly. Such was, of course, the case with regard to the Bolsheviks' takeover in 1917. Compared to the disillusioning processes of the First World War, the revolution in Russia seemed lucid and clear-cut. There was also a romanticism about the Bolshevik revolution that, in Western European eyes, had much to do with the vastness, mystery, and primitivism of Russia itself. Eventually, the revolution in Russia lost its romantic appeal. Once Stalinization set in, forced industrialization took precedence over human liberation, and the Soviet Union emerged playing the old power game with a new deck of cards (deceptively marked "Communist Ideology"), revolutionary consciousness in Western Europe has shifted over toward the romantic allure of the civil war in Spain and subsequent revolutions in China, Cuba, Algeria, Southeast Asia, and so on. The romantic allure here is akin to the nineteenth century's passionate sympathy for nationalistic uprisings, such as the one in Greece. The revolutionary movement has become, especially in the non-Western world where it is now centered, inextricably intertwined with movements of national self-determination, although this is a notable departure from the Russian prototype of 1917.

After the First World War, those who encountered in its fullness the dilemma of revolutionary consciousness had to deal with an entirely new agenda, having nothing to do with nineteenth century categories. The social changes that became evident at the war's end are part of the fabric of the alteration in revolutionary consciousness. The simple fact of the survival of bourgeois regimes and capitalist systems—in spite of the evidence that placed the blame for the war itself at their very doorsteps—necessitated a return to the revolutionary drawing boards, and an upping of the stakes as well. The decimation of the generations of youthful males, especially those born between 1885 and 1900, increased the participation of females in Western European economic and political life. In most countries, women's suffrage was secured immediately after the war's end. This pacified the feminist challenge that had been on the rise in the decades before the war. It was indicative of the broadening of the parameters of injustice and inequality in the industrialized world. After the First World War a proliferation of possibilities, and a panoply of pluralisms came increasingly to characterize life in the industrialized societies. This increase influenced the Left as well, producing what might be called the simultaneous expansion and decentralization of the revolutionary idea. This development, in turn, loosened the strict identification of the revolutionary idea with the material aims of the oppressed proletariat. This enlarged revolutionary theme, if underrepresented at first, became central to the concerns of the New Left from the late 1950s on. Hence, the dilemmas of the menially employed and the unsklilled are subsumed by the repressive tensions weighing upon those solidly rooted in the middle class itself. The shift thus has been away from the view of the middle class as necessarily an enemy (from which only a few individuals can set themselves apart) toward a broader understanding of oppression and deprivation. This shift has been marked to some degree by a psychologizing of the notion of deprivation. To a great extent, however, the concept itself still remains tangled and enmeshed in the idea of materialism, in which it originated conceptually.

By 1924, the Soviet regime proclaimed its pursuit of "socialism in one country." This was yet another sign of variation and rupture in the nineteenth-century Marxist revolutionary orthodoxy, which had foreseen the revolution developing cataclysmically, internationally, spreading like wildfire, and enveloping every tottering timber that supported the bourgeois society. Yet also, in association with the proclamation of abandoning worldwide revolution in favor of concentrating on socialism's development in the USSR, the genuine liberalization of society was abandoned in the Soviet Union. The New Economic Policy that provided for what may be roughly described as a mixed economy (some state ownership, modest collectivization, and significant private ownership) from 1922 to 1927 was the basis of a society that was authentically free in many ways—culturally, intellectually, in terms of both social and sexual relationships, as well as educationally, and so on. This provided the basis of a social order that was neither monolithic nor totalitarian, pointing to the fact that it is perhaps more the demands of technology and economic organization that yield homogenization than political ideas themselves.

The cultural activity in the Soviet Union during and immediately following the Civil War bore witness to the richness of socialist cultural life and the fact that it was, in principle, as free as the cultural life in any other sort of society. It laid the basis in fact for many subsequent theoretical arguments. It marked a period of genuine freedom, in artistic life at least, that was to become unknown in the Soviet Union after 1930 and, by extension, suppressed—except in rare and brief instances—through all of Eastern Europe since 1948.

The 1920s in Western Europe were a decade of numerous influences, various trajectories, the inspiration of America for the first time (jazz and Hollywood movies), artistic *cum* intellectual movements of enormous psychological dimension in surrealism and expressionism, and the breaking forth of numerous new possibilities, such as radio. The impact of new forms within the general framework of a pluralistic society influenced all aspects of Western European life, including the Left. This effervescence led to what might be called a decentralizing of the political Left, and the burgeoning of a variety of postures and perspectives. There was, among other things, a sense that the strict association of the Left's program with the oppressed working class might need overhauling. This overhaul did not really come about on a grand scale until the end of the 1950s. Then the New Left abandoned the rigid identification with the oppressed laboring classes in favor of a wider definition of oppression, while more cautious Leftists reframed their ideology as "Eurocommunism," seeking to make communist parties into broad-based popular parties whose appeals cut across class lines. The growth of the Left in sheer numbers meant a qualitative growth in the variety of perspectives on the Left. "Socialism in one country" in the Soviet Union, in spite of the problematic role the U.S.S.R. played for leftists everywhere, meant endorsement of the notion—Marx's originally—that the path to socialism might take different forms in different places. This endorsement meant, too, that attitudes toward an appropriate revolutionary culture would become more accommodating to variety as time passed.

It was within the widening parameters of what means might be suitable to enacting one's stance on the Left that Bertolt Brecht explored the possibilities of committed, revolutionary dramatic writing. One of his earliest plays, *Drums in the Night* (1922), was similar to Toller's *Mass Man* in both theme and mood. Yet initially Becht needs to be acknowledged as a figure whose concept of theater was as important to revolutionary consciousness as was any specific embodiment of that consciousness to which his writing itself attained.

From the late nineteenth century, perhaps even more strongly in drama than in narrative prose, naturalism had become a predominant mode before the First World War. This naturalism had at its core, most often, the underscoring of the "social message" of deprivation, dehumanization, hypocrisy, injustice, and bourgeois shallowness. In Germany, in the second half of the 1920s a "new objectivity" or naturalism was on the rise. Brecht reacted by conceiving of theatrical means which tended in the opposite direction. In the "alienation effect" he sought simultaneously to justify and to enact situations in which the audience reacts to problems presented in the material of the drama and reaches a decision about them. With denaturalized sets, with language that departs from naturalistic idiom and voice (in the direction, often, of a mock-epic quality), and by the introduction of music and song, the elements of alienation are achieved. They produce, when taken together, a presence that goes beyond sentimentality, identification, and empathy—the ostensible mainstays of representational art. Here the work of art becomes a vehicle for ideas that may be decided on the basis of ideology.

Brecht's *Saint Joan of the Stockyards* (1929) is set in a fantasized Chicago. The female protagonist, Joan Dark, is an organizer for the Salvation Army. She cares about the poor. She makes no connection, however, between her own charitable good intentions and her relationship to the system that perpetuates the needs she wishes to redress. The play is an exercise in her own consciousness raising.

Joan is still proclaiming that goodness exists as army machine guns are trained on striking workers in the stockyards. Her transformation is, however, swift. As the meat packers chant on behalf of their deepest wish—unification of business and the human soul—Joan is accepting her own radicalization. It is dehumanization that she recognizes as the stage beyond, yet inevitably rooted in, poverty. Accepting this awareness is not easy for her. Finally, she follows out its consequences logically, proclaiming: "Only force helps where force rules, and / Only men help where men are." Her own transformation is juxtaposed against the cyclical processes of industrial capitalism, all duly noted and reported as background to the action: production; prosperity; downturn; depression; poverty. Insecurity reigns everywhere, inherent as it is in the system itself. Only the devious "doing business" of the packers and the speculator Mauler on the one hand, and the transcendant opiates of the army of salvationists on the other, hold back the recognition of what truly is.

There is an intrusion of a loudspeaker voice in the action. It brings snippets of what in the modern world is called "news": "POUND FALLS! BANK OF ENGLAND CLOSES! . . . EIGHT MILLION UNEMPLOYED IN U.S.A.! FIVE-YEAR PLAN SUCCEEDS! BRAZIL POURS COFFEE CROP INTO OCEAN! . . . BATTLE BETWEEN POLICE AND UNEMPLOYED OUTSIDE HENRY FORD'S PLANT IN DETROIT! BIGGEST EUROPEAN TRUST, MATCH TRUST, GOES BANKRUPT!"

In this staccato the play reaches a crescendo. It joins itself to external "history," it takes its side with Moscow in optimism as regards the "Five-Year Plan," it plays out the irrationality and internal contradiction that is assumed to be inherent in the capitalist system. It points to the randomness and the disjointedness of the industrial, financial, political and social complexities of life in modern industrial capitalism.

In 1932, Brecht wrote the screenplay and Slatan Dudow directed a motion picture financed by the Communist party in Germany. *Kuhle Wampe* took its title from the name of a makeshift emergency community set up by the unemployed on the outskirts of Berlin in 1932. Filmed when unemployment in Germany was reaching 20 percent (exactly equaling the figure for the United States, where the Great Depression had begun three years earlier), the narrative celebrates youthful exuberance and hope. In the mode of the expressive realist films produced in the Soviet Union during the 1920s, individual characterizations are downplayed in favor of narrative situations in which the solidarity, vitality, and collective awareness of the group are emphasized. Here is portrayal of a consciousness that is completely expunged of the pathos, the pity, and the misery of the naturalistic mode, in spite of being situationally a dramatic piece in which the characters confront the most dire and threatening of economic conditions. In the next-to-last scene of the narrative, a number of young men and women from Kuhle Wampe are traveling by subway in Berlin. A typical bourgeois, who is reading his newspaper and commenting loudly on its contents, begins to argue with one of the young unemployed workers. The point of departure for their argument is a published report of the government's destruction of a portion of the coffee crop in Brazil. The bourgeois responds to this by talking of "us," meaning the German people as a national collective whole, and hence speaking of "our" interests in the matter! The young man responds to this with combined incredulity and hostility. Does "we" mean "you" and "me," all of us together and with some sort of shared interest? This is delusive; it is false consciousness; it is nationalistic consciousness, which not only ignores, but patently denies, the differences between social classes and, further, between the measure and merit of their particular self-interests as determined from the basis of class identity. The notion of common national interest is a sham. Their argument ends; the subway train arrives in a station; the young people from Kuhle Wampe detrain. Arm in arm, shoulder to shoulder, they march through the subway station, the words they are singing echoing through the underground tunnels: "FORWARD, FORGETTING NOTHING! FORWARD, AND NEVER FORGET! JUST WHOSE CITY IS THIS CITY? JUST WHOSE WORLD IS THIS WORLD?"

From one perspective, the work of art relying upon the alienation effect might be seen as a theatrical throwback to the flattened allegorical characters, the didacticism, and the moralizing of the religious drama of the Middle Ages. There is nothing necessarily pejorative implied in such an observation. The phenomena of the "happening," street theater, the extending of the theaterical stage so that the barrier between audience and cast is eliminated, and the blending of performance with work of art and of spectatorship with performance all trace back to pre-Renaissance models. There is, after all, a residual atavism in that element of modern and contemporary consciousness that is revolutionary, and that is self-consciously politicized. That atavism suggests the connecting links of community, of brotherhood (and sisterhood, as well!), of the human substance of pre-modern and folkish societies insofar as they were pre-capitalist and hence free from the inherent irrationality, the dehumanization, and alienation of the human condition within a capitalist framework.

The influences of a theater of alienating effects (mingling more recently with the devices of the theater of the absurd) have been rife in Western Europe since the Second World War. Eventually these have entered the cinema, in French productions of the mid-1960s and then, with a vengeance, in great numbers of movies produced in the German Federal Republic during the 1970s. Perhaps the best instance of enactment of the combination of Brechtian techniques (updated and elaborated upon) with the dimensions of revolutionary consciousness itself has been Peter Weiss's *The Persecution and Assassination of Jean-Paul Marat as Performed by the Inmates of the Asylum of Charenton under the Direction of the Marquis de Sade* (1963).

The play counterpoints the dialectic between the social rebel Marat and the individualistic rebel Sade. Marat: "There is a rioting mob inside me / Simone / I am the Revolution"; Sade: "For me the only reality is the imagination / The world inside miyself / The Revolution no longer interests me." Sade is obsessed with knowing the self, with the authentic rebellion that exists only in the individual's imagination. He rebels against nature, seeing the ultimate rebellion as murder. By contrast, Marat sees political and social action as ways of endowing nature with meaning. Says Marat, "I never believed the pen alone / Could destroy institutions." Marat sees the problem of the revolution as the inability of the masses to obliterate history, to destroy everything, and to start over again. By contrast, Sade maintains that equality actually leads to loss of freedom.

The confusion throughout the piece between reality and illusion dates back to the romantics and the drama of Georg Büchner (especially *Woyzek*, 1836). Interest in the reality/illusion conflict was rekindled at the beginning of the twentieth century, with great attention to dreams. *Marat/Sade* updates the challenging of external experience—an oblique attack upon the intellectual presumptions of rationalism and empiricism—beyond the duality of the dream and the real world. This goes, too, beyond the 1920s' expressionist fascination with distortion and pathology as projections of interior psychic states. In this play, in fact, distortion and pathology are as much a part of the observable world, the real world, the "environing world," as are any other of the phenomena of experience.

Marat/Sade is set in an insane asylum. The setting and other elements are like *The Physicists*, by Friedrich Dürrenmatt (1953), which explores the responsibility of the scientist for his ideas by reference to the tension between two historical personages, Newton and Einstein. These are the identities taken on by two actual physicists who have incarcerated themselves and who then commit murder in order to prevent their ideas from being exploited and costing many more lives.

Marat/Sade develops the long-standing Western device of the play within a play, as well as being suffused with allusions and random enactments drawn from folk art traditions, such as mime, popular music, and the circus. The time frame of *Marat/Sade* may be called three-dimensional: it draws together and overlaps two historic events that are not historically concurrent: de Sade's incarceration and Marat's role in the French Revolution.

Moreover, the thematic material of *Marat/Sade* relates directly to the topic explored by Albert Camus in his long essay published first in 1951, *The Rebel*. That book was greeted with derision and scorn by critics on the Left, for it portrayed what might be called existential revolt as more fundamentally human than—and implicitly superior to—what Camus labels as historical revolt. Camus saw historical revolt, the modern materialist revolutionary project, as only a surface reflection of one aspect of rebellion, which is inherent in the human condition. For all humans are endowed with a propensity to rebel against that paradox that is fundamental to life. On the one hand, we can never know enough about the "others" in whose company we find ourselves, and we can never—in spite of herculean efforts to do so—make sense out of the world of the "others" in which we find ourselves, namely society. In contrast to this, however, we all know something we might wish to purge from awareness, and that is that we shall die. Although we do not comprehend the meaning of our mortality, we are clearly aware of it.

In *The Rebel* Albert Camus tried to distinguish between this propensity to rebellion that is inherent in the human condition and the choice of involvement in political revolutionary movements that is situational. Camus might be said then to have drawn a sharp line between existential rebellion and historical revolution. That separation is, by contrast, blurred in several novels of André Malraux, dating from the late 1920s and the 1930s.

In the earliest of these novels, *The Conquerors* (1927), the setting is China and the subject is that combination of culture, talent, and logic that defines the committed European revolutionary. The character Borodin, who is portrayed sketchily, is the epitome of cautious strategy and discipline. His personality and temprament are definitive of the technocratic Bolshevik, for whom the cause is beyond challenge. The more complex protagonist is Garine, essentially a metaphysical or existential rebel who has found the Left—yet who may also find it wanting. To Borodin, Garine's individualism is a bourgeois sickness from which the victim cannot recover. To phrase it in other language, as the American critic Edmund Wilson once did, the character Garine "has a certain alloy of old-fashioned romanticism."

Part of Garine's dilemma is that he has feelings for humanity, especially for the beaten and the down-trodden, but he also has an awareness of his own personal quest for power. A complicating factor is the ideological conflict between Garine and Borodin. In his attempt to resolve his inner sense of alienation, Garine has committed himself to the communist revolution in China. He wants to identify with it and to make himself a part of it. Borodin, a Russian, is detached from the Chinese revolution itself; his essential commitment is to his participation in it as a strategist for policies made in Moscow. Garine has fashioned himself psychologically into a free agent, one who has chosen-in-consciousness to make of himself what he wills. Yet when it comes to action that lies beyond the realm of psychological posturing, Garine is immersed in conflict. Borodin is disciplined, and hence a man of action. Those actions, however, are not the dictates of his own will. Garine is comparatively free, yet thwarted from taking action.

Courage is not the issue in *The Conquerors*. It is difficult to argue with the cold-blooded comment by the Soviet agent Nicolaeff that there is no courage in the world that can sustain a ten-minute session with "an experienced interrogator." The would-be adventurer and conqueror Garine is in search of a meaning that lies well beyond the exercise of either duty or courage. In the Revolution he is pursuing meaning and the making of sense out of committed experience. Garine has fled Europe and headed eastwards after being judged guilty in a trial (on a charge of helping women to obtain abortions) that he has called "absurd." Once again, as so often in a vision that infuses Western consciousness since the publication of *Heart of Darkness*, the wanderer has left his milieu in search of self-realization through cultural and philosophical reappraisal.

On the surface, Garine succeeds. The success is, however, empty. Were this emptiness understood strictly as resulting from Garine's inner frustration that the quest for value and meaning still has not been satisfied by participation in the revolutionary process, this would be interesting at the level of individual awareness only. The telling issue is that the impulse to a rebel's life, in which the option of revolutionary commitment is chosen, is itself problematic. The appeal of the revolutionary ethos—especially after Marx's claims that it is both scientific and imbued with historical inevitability—is that it offers meaning. For the revolution to be both empirically demonstrable and necessitated by history itself militates against absurdity and meaninglessness. Compassion and humaneness are surely wellsprings of revolutionary commitment. Beyond them, however, is the undeniable appeal of Marxist and neo-Marxist analyses, which offer a dazzling intellectual construct through which the most complex of social relations are rendered intelligible and correctable.

Alas, the dilemma of the individual revolutionary is inseparable from the dilemma of revolution itself. If the revolutionary process cannot provide liberation from alienation and meaningless to someone who is committed to it, then how can the revolution triumphant liberate humankind from the yoke of injustice and irrationality? If the revolution offers no clear salvation from the abyss of nihilism to its participants, how can we count on the revolution's capacity for redirecting human experience into rational meaning and value later on? Marxism, and the various strands of neo-Marxism, offer hope, promise, and a measure of certitude about the eventual triumph of the proletariat revolution that will lead to a classless and stateless society. That optimism, which is an aspect of the modern Left's appeal, becomes a source of disillusionment in the face of failure and frustration.

Another novel by Malraux, in English entitled *Man's Fate*, was completed in 1933. Like *The Conquerors*, its setting is China. The course of action follows a form of literary neorealism that looks and sounds journalistic. Its cast of characters emphasizes the internationalism of the revolution. Their array of tempraments, typologies, and personalities permits, moreover, an exploration of the complex choices faced by revolutionaries.

Early in the novel, young Tchen is carrying out a mission whereby he must murder a sleeping man in order to get hold of a bill of sale that the revolutionaries need to acquire armaments. As he hovers over the man's bed, he is suddenly moved to first plunge the knife into his own arm. Doing so somehow relieves his anguish, and he completes the work assigned to him by the party. Yet, that act on orders provides the psychological basis for Tchen's later choice of anarchism. On his own, he plans to assassinate Chiang Kai-shek (the Nationalist leader then precariously allied with the Chinese Communists). He throws a hand bomb at a passing car in which he has calculated Chiang Kai-shek is riding, then shoots himself on the spot. He dies without recognizing that he has targeted the wrong car, in which only innocents are traveling. The terrorist, driven increasingly by rage at injustice and by impatience at the slow pace of change, is a particular type of revolutionary. In Europe terrorism proper has been most notable among revolutionaries in the decades before the First World War (with anarchist bombings) and in the years from the late 1960s to the early 1980s (with kidnappings and "kneecappings" gaining precedence over bombings). Yet resort to illicit force is a staple of revolutionary action. Whether the violence is justified as a strategic tactic or is random and arbitrary makes little difference morally. The debate over calculated violence as opposed to the spontaneous and sporadic sort is a peculiar subprovince of modern and contemporary political theory.

The most important character in *Man's Fate* is Kyo Gisors. The cause of his estrangement from society—and his particular mark of being an outcast—is that he is a "half-breed": the son of a French father and a Japanese mother. Gisors, after leading a brief communist takeover of Shanghai, is eventually defeated. He is captured and imprisoned and dies in imprisonment. In contrast to Garine of *The Conquerors*, who succeeds but comes up empty-handed spiritually, Gisors fails, but triumphs psychologically. As the historian James D.

Wilkinson has pointed out in his analysis of this novel in relation to Malraux's political thought, Kyo Gisors may be called a "Bolshevik hero." Wilkinson is quick to point out, however, that he means "Bolshevik" not historically, but culturally. This Bolshevik hero is a "human type who combines enormous energy with a humanitarian ideal." The designation has nothing to do with the Russian political faction that made the second stage of the revolution in 1917, save that the original Bolshevik ideal (soon betrayed by the Stalinists) was based on this form of heroism. Gisors's revolutionary commitment has produced in him an abiding sense of solidarity, both with other humans for whom he feels sympathy and for the cause itself for which he gives his life.

While the representational works of revolutionary consciousness dating from the 1930s explore issues of revolutionary commitment that are perennial, they were written in a specific and a highly charged milieu. Fascism was solidly established in Italy before the end of the 1920s; Hitler became chancellor of Germany at the beginning of 1933, and Nazi power was consolidated there within a year; the Spanish Civil War ended in 1939 with the victory of Generalissimo Francisco Franco, supported by the extremist right-wing Falange. In the Soviet Union Stalin's campaign for forced industrialization had begun with proclamation of the First Five-Year Plan in 1927, ushering in an era in which state terror flourished against the land-owning peasants, undesirables were exiled to Siberia, and old-line Bolsheviks whose scruples would not permit them to surrender qucikly enough to the technocratic and bureaucratic pronouncements were purged. Between the rise of the totalitarian Right and the emerging evidence of betrayal of the Revolution by Stalin and his cohorts, the Western European leftists found themselves squeezed. Given these circumstances, antipathy toward Stalinism was blocked from reaching full expression in Western Europe. For there is in modern Western thought a residual presence of central concern that dates at least to the Romantic era of the nineteenth century. André Malraux himself was referring to it, it seems, when he was quoted at the 1934 Soviet Writers' Congress as saying, "If Marxism is the consciousness of the social, culture is the consciousness of the psychological."

Ignazio Silone's novel *Bread and Wine* (1936) was written during Silone's exile from Italian fascism. The novel's protagonist, Pietro Spina, has sought refuge-in-hiding in a small mountain village in the impoverished Abruzzi region of southern Italy. He is a thinker and Communist, but as a disguise he has chosen to wear a priest's habit. Perhaps the garments themselves have little to do with it, but progressively Spina seems absorbed with questions of spirituality and of meaning and value. His revolutionary credo, if not taken over, is at least tentatively subverted by these thoughts and reflections. Of course, the prophetic value in the elements of tension between Communism and Catholicism suggested in the novel cannot be denied. By the end of the Second World War, the notion of Communist and Catholic unity in the Resistance had become believable, if still fraught with tension. Hence the protagonist embodies in his person the antithetical elements which have evidently found more integration in Italy since 1945 than anywhere else: the revolutionary Left and the Catholic faith.

Throughout the work, Spina (playing the role of Don Paolo) is engaged not so much in revolutionary work as in observation of the peasants in whose midst he is hiding. The superstition, simplicity, and earthiness of the peasant mentality, as reflected through the mind's eye of the sophisticated revolutionary, is the central subject of the book. The region itself is cast descriptively as isolated, abandoned, and alienated from "civilized" modern Italy. For the civilized ones the modes of accommodation, good sense, and rational behavior lead most clearly toward acquiescence to fascism. The single exception is young Murica. Temporarily he gives in to police torture and agrees to inform on his comrades. Later arrested again, however, he refuses to repudiate his antifascism. The police crown him with a chamberpot, place a broomstick in his hand as a scepter, and then wrap him in a large red rug and beat him to death.

Both novels by Malraux, as well as Silone's *Bread and Wine*, explore the dimensions of the revolution and the revolutionary—in opposition, in struggle, and in flight. *Darkness at Noon*, written between 1938 and 1940 by Arthur Koestler, considers the revolution triumphant. The protagonist in *Darkness at Noon* is Rubashov, a composite of those Old Bolsheviks who were tried during the Soviet purges from 1934 to 1938. This is hardly a "roman à clef"; none of the characters parallels a "real-life" historical figure on a precise one-to-one basis.

The reader first encounters Rubashov as he is being arrested. In his cell he begins a long, rambling recollection of his own career in the revolution and in service to the party. As it turns out, a few years earlier Rubashov had been arrested in Hitler's Germany by Gestapo agents. He draws an association between that arrest and this one, between those agents of the Nazis and the secret police in the state dominated by his own party, between Hitler and the Soviet Union's own Number One (Stalin). The perception of these parallels drawn into consciousness by Rubashov are in accord with the point of view that developed roughly a decade later, in the early 1950s. That was to look at Hitler and Stalin as alter egos to each other, and to view nazism and bolshevism as reverse sides of the same totalitarian coin.

For Rubashov, however, the issue is touched with nostalgia for the intellectual excitement and rigor of the prerevolutionary years. In a way, this can be seen as an aging humanist's yearing for "the way we were," for the high-minded sense of inquiry and pursuit of justice that preceded the party's coming to power and its eventual dependency on technocrats and neanderthalers once it had gotten there. The "new" Soviet men are emptied of compassion and emptied of spirit. They are materialists pure and simple, with no perception of the broader goals of human equality and justice that lie beyond.

Yet Rubashov is not self-delusive. He knows that he too, in the past, has sacrificed others to the revolution, to the cause, and to the party. He has sacrificed others to the foreign policy of the Soviet Union, as a consequence of his belief that history is on its side. He reflects upon this, in moods of both anxiety and reverie; yet he can in no way resolve the dilemmas confronting him.

In the name of what, after all, is duplicity, terror, and murder justified? This would become a question for essayists immediately after the Second World War, who in Western Europe would sometimes answer that the Soviet Union posed a special case: that because of the promise communism held for humanity, the Soviet Union was justified in the terror it had unleashed on its citizens. Nowhere was this point of view argued more extensively and compellingly than in the French essayist Maurice Merleau-Ponty's *Humanism and Terror* (1947), although Jean-Paul Sartre and several others took up the argument as well.

Floods kill; diseases kill; catastrophes of nature and accidents of all sorts kill. Why then should not murder be used for human ends, and in the advancement of clear, justifiable, and historically determined goals? In the words of Ivanov, the interrogator of Rubashov and the novel's representative of the new Soviet order: "Your Roskolnikov [referring to Dostoyevsky's character, who is a favorite of Rubashov's] is, however, a fool and a criminal; not because he behaves logically in killing the old woman, but because he is doing it in his personal interest. The principle that the ends justifies the means is and remains the only rule of political ethics; anything else is just vague chatter and melts away between one's fingers." And in this consciousness is contained the means of condemning not only egoistic and self-indulgent acts of protest and criminality, but wrong ideas as well: "Each wrong idea . . . is a crime committed against future generations. Therefore we have to punish wrong ideas as others punish crimes: with death."

Several issues conflict here. Not the least among them is Rubashov's eventual decision to admit to crimes that he has not even committted and to make one final sacrifice, an ultimate one, for the party. This is a reasoned and a conscious choice. Rubashov has not been broken by the conditions of his imprisonment and the harshness of his interrogations. On the contrary, it is clear that he has maintained his intellectual and emotional strength and integrity throughout. He opts instead for the final decision that is consistent with authenticity of the destiny he had chosen long before, when he made his commitment-in-consciousness to the revolution. This is a logical extension of his sense of a final duty to the party, and his final service to the highest goals of the internationalist revolutionary idea.

For many readers in the Western world, outside of those whose sympathies lie unequivocally on the side of the Left, this ending is difficult to assimilate. At stake, of course, is not simply how one judges Stalinism and Soviet society but rather how the myth of revolutionary change is challenged here. For what authentic alternatives exist to enforced change in many instances; for what ends are which means justified; and where is there ever a revolution that does not devour its children or a social order founded on certain ideals that does not, at some point and in some manner, seriously betray or ignore them?

Revolutionary consciousness has waxed and waned in Western Europe with the course of events. Beyond that ebb and flow, however, the Left has retained in the twentieth century a surprisingly resilient and consistent perspective that broadly informs various dimensions of experience. The course of the Second World War, brought on as it was by the rise of Hitler and characterized by partisan struggles in resistance to the German occupation, resulted in an eventual Soviet military victory (even though Stalin waited until after the Germans attacked to "go to war against fascism"). Politically, diplomatically, and spiritually, the Soviet reputation was at a high point in 1945. Throughout Western Europe communists were often in good standing because of their participation—often valorous and usually unfailing—in the resistance movements across the continent. In France an old, traditionalist, national patriotic conservative—De Gaulle—took French communists into his post war government. In Italy Roberto Rossellini's neorealist film *Open City* (1944) highlighted the nexus of cooperation between Catholics and Communists in the partisan struggle against nazism and the German Occupation.

The Holocaust on the one hand, and the atomic bombing of Hiroshima and Nagasaki on the other, contributed to creating a situation that in the minds of many artists demanded an art of engagement. Linking art with moral and political responsibility was nothing new. Doing so on the Left had motivated the avant-garde even before the Second World War. Since 1945, with the stakes for human survival having been raised exponentially by the coming of the atomic age, and with generalized liberation and freedom of expression growing throughout the Western world, the felt moral imperative of creating an art of political and social commitment has expanded. In turn, this increased sensitivity to the creation of an art of moral and political engagement has helped foster the return of the word "ideology" to its original meaning. In the nineteenth century, for Destutt de Tracy (who coined the phrase) or for Karl Marx (who often used it), "ideology" meant a cluster of attitudes and values. During the years between the First and the Second world wars the term was distorted, perhaps, to descibe only a coherent sociopolitical program. In some quarters, this misusage still prevails. "Ideology" refers not to a program but to a construct-in-consciousness shared by some number of people who form a collectivity, about the nature, value, and meaning of the public and collective dimensions of human experience.

This shift to the original meaning of ideology coincides with the search for more open-ended and individualistic positions, particularly on the Left. After long term apparent compromise with Soviet communism, the traditional Left in Western Europe was quickly superseded after 1956 by the appearance of the New Left. As Roland Stromberg has pointed out, the manifestations known as the New Left of the 1960s were in the making long before the U.S. military involvement in Viet-Nam became a catalyst for youthful protest, both in North America and Western Europe.

The New Left has had no single, coherent ideology. The traditional Left was, by contrast, inextricably linked with Soviet perversions of the communist worldview. Moreover, the emergence of the New Left was as much a phenomenon of politics in Western Europe struggling toward greater self-identity and independence, as it was a matter of change in ideology. It marked the leftists' own rebellion against Soviet domination, much as, about the same time, the conservative Charles DeGaulle led the rebellion of the political Right against the American version of order, stability, and freedom. The New Left originated then as a Western European response to the excesses and weaknesses of Soviet ideology, and was marked by a turning to heroes in the non-Western world: Mao, Castro, Ché, Ho Chi Minh. It turned its attention to and manifested support for national liberation movements all over the world. Tacitly, it implied that the proletarian cause in most developed Western societies is a complex, not a simple, matter. Although the "working classes" have remained, indeed, a source of concern, they have generally ceased to be a source of inspiration. The New Left has accepted the historical burden that the ideology of revolutionary consciousness is primarily fostered and responded to by disaffected and alienated elements of the bourgeoisie itself. Hence, the New Left has accepted a broader, and more meaningful, definition of alienation: a definition that accorded far better with the so-called modernist versions of a multidimensional and shoreless alienation that knows no boundaries and no strict distinctions as to class or the simple relationship of individuals to the product of their labor. The collective psychology of the New Left is oral, as opposed to the inherent anality of the Old Left. Here is revolution with a strong libido, signs of desire for transcendence, a quasi-literate passion for the shout and the slogan at the evident expense of dialectics or any other form of deductive exposition. The surrealist passion to shock the "respectables" seemed of scant usefulness to the Communist parties of the 1920s. Such posturing meshed better with the sense of liberation and personal gratification found in Wilhelm Reich's renegade push for sexual liberation, seeking to cure society of the wickedness unleashed upon the world, many times over, by bad orgasm. The New Left promoted a kind of existential protest in favor of individual choice as a radical category of awareness, and against all bureaucratic and corporate forms. It praised immediacy and situationality—qualities of a semi-existentialist authenticity—against strategy, party programs, and dialectical trivialization; it sought immediate peace terms with nature and an assault on technology in general, making it look, at times, like an escapist romanticism to end all romanticism.

The proletarian myth, which had perhaps reached its peak and found its most pervasive expression in mimetic works of the 1930s, underwent revision. Alan Sillitoe's novel *Saturday Night and Sunday Morning* (1958) portrays the hedonistic self-liberation of Arthur Seaton, whose authenticity goes well beyond the trade union mentality and whose rebelliousness takes forms of which a great number would be disapproved by self-styled progressives:

> "If you're Arthur Seaton, working man, you pit your muscles and your guts against the precision-machine lathe five days a week. Monday to Friday you live in the factory reek of oil-suds and shaved steel. Payday comes, and you pocket your boodle, minus a load for the damn taxes. You vaguely long to blow up The Establishment, but suddenly—it's Saturday night . . ."

As Arthur says (bursting with energy, yet channeling it into his machismo and having it in turn channeled into his own consumerism), "It's a great life if you don't weaken." The down-to-earth situation of Arthur is beyond a mere indulgent naturalism rooted in self-pity. ". . . [T]he big wide world hasn't heard from you yet, no, not by a long way, though it won't be long now."

The guy who has something to tell the world and the chant that the chorus repeats throughout *Marat/Sade*, "What is a revolution without general copulation?"—these are elements of the New Left. Arthur's sense of presence in the world becomes, a decade after the publication of *Saturday Night and Sunday Morning*, the slogan painted on a wall near the Sorbonne in 1968: "We want the world, and we want it now." The chant from *Marat/Sade* reflects the self-conscious libidinal path to recognition and meaning often taken since. Both are shouts against a world of meaninglessness and alienation, which only marginally are outcomes of economic conditions.

The revolutionary ethos of hard, partisan work, sacrifice, and idelogoical purity becomes a distant memory in eclipse. It is just that in Alain Resnais's film *The War is Over* (1966). The protagonist, Diego Mora (played by Yves Montand), has spent three decades in service to the leftist cause, dating back to the Civil War in Spain. He shuttles back and forth between Spain and France, between his own long-term optimism and his inevitable sense of disappointment, and between two women. *The War Is Over* reaffirms, eventually, the commitment to patience, work, and the assimilation of disappointment as necessary to authentic political change. Its optimism does not stop there, however, nor does its subtlety. Diego finds reaffirmation in the political vocation to which he has given his life, and fullness and satisfaction in his romance with Marianne. This unity is visualized when their images merge on the screen, but do so from the point of view of each other.

The revolutionary consciousness in *The War Is Over* is mature, patient, optimistic—but it is hardly simple-minded, crudely proletarianized, or simplistically counter-cultural. The commitment here is to continuing, to hoping, and to building. These values are counterpointed well, and eventually reinforced, in a film by Gillo Pontecorvo from the same year: *The Battle of Algiers.*

The Battle of Algiers looks and feels to the viewer as if it were a documentary film. It has the appearances of reportage: the graininess of fast-speed black-and-white film-stock; the tentative angles and focuses of the hand-held camera; the spontaneity of action and motivation of individuals whose energies are collective; the setting up of specific shots and sequences laced through with a sensibility of randomness. As fictional narrative film, however, it embraces the emotionality of the revolutinary cause of the national Liberation Front in Algeria. The themes, techniques, and devices here borrow from the Italian neorealist cinema of the years immediately after the Second World War. The rhythms, the characterizations, and the editing suggest influences of the Soviet expressive realist movies of the 1920s.

The fictional portrayal places the revolutionary Ali-la-Pointe in opposition to the Frenchman Matthieu. It is likely that the choice of "Matthieu" as the Frenchman's name relates to Sartre's fictional hero of the three-novel trilogy "The Road to Freedom." In *The Battle of Algiers* it is the situation itself from which there is no exit. The consequences on both sides of an issue derive directly from the initial choices; these become, increasingly, choices from which there is no escape. There is a never-ending spiral toward the slogan (borrowed from Hegel) that produces the Sartrean "You cannot choose not to choose" writ large, collectively in terms of one's own inextricable oneness with the government, the party, the program, or the linkages of history itself. When the New Left proclaims, "You are either with us or against us," then it has not only emotion but moral reason on its side.

When the Algerian rebel Hassiba plants a bomb at a European café, only her glance around reflects her humanity and her anguish. The medium carries the moral message. Yet the differences between the two sides do not simply come down to a gamble, with the course of history as the stakes. The National Liberation Front, seemingly defeated at first, is able to draw upon its own emotional and energetic continuity, so that the struggle goes on, is never ending, passes from one phase to another, and perhaps retreats, but does not degenerate destructively. This is the living out of the Old Left slogan of Lenin himself—"One step forward, two steps back"—updated and realized in its non-Western setting.

An important aspect in Western European mimetic works since the early 1960s has been the self-conscious examination of the conflicts, paradoxes, and dilemmas confronted by the Left. The tensions inherent in and underlying the contemporary revolutionary posture are explored, for example, in two motion pictures, *Masculine/Feminine* (1966) and *La Chinoise* (1967), both directed by Jean-Luc Godard. The former maintains most of the conventions of narrative film, and much of the tempo and content of cinema verité. *Masculine/Feminine* portrays the youthful generation of the 1960s: the children of Karl Marx and Coca-Cola. *Masculine/Feminine* itself is a coda for the dialectic that exists between the sexes, which is the core of what are called sexual politics. This dynamic is presented through the convoluted relationship of Paul, a young man of comfortable background with a social conscience and a passion for politics, and Madeleine, a "Yé-Yé" singer awash in that amalagam known as the Euro-American youth culture. At one point, Paul's questioning her, primarily about politics, is set off with the introductory title: "Dialogue with a Consumer Product." Paul possesses all the potential of an acutely aware and committed activist. His problem is the problem that faces every would-be revolutionary in contemporary society. That is how one overcomes the myths and seductions of a romanticization of life that is now carried not in the individual soul but in magazines and films, on television and billboards.

La Chinoise is predicated on the more direct cinematic exploration of the issues confronting (and confining) revolutionary consciousness. The movie is identified in its full title as being in the process of "making itself." That was the very stage of revolutionary consciousness itself in Western Europe by the late 1960s. The unifying element of the movie is the cell of young people who call themselves the "Aden-Arabie." The name of the group is taken from a novel written by Paul Nizan just before World War I. The five are students on summer vacation, and their revolutionary stronghold is a vacation cottage "expropriated" from the upper-middle-class parents of one of their friends.

Clearly, *La Chinoise* is primarily critical of the contradictions implied by these students playing at revolution. Yet it also explores the genuine tension generated by the contradictions involved in manifesting revolutionary action in contemporary circumstances. In one scene, Veronique and Guillaume, two members of the summer season collective, sit side by side—he reading from Chairman Mao's *Little Red Book* and she from the writings of the Marquis de Sade. This fleeting image points once more, as did the dramatic work *Marat/Sade*, to the ego/erotic nexus of revolutionary impulse that is so highly developed in the Western world. At its most perceptive moments, the New Left has grasped the fact that revolutionary consciousness in contemporary circumstances must come to grips somehow with the bridging of materialist goals of equality and spiritual goals of self-fulfillment.

Throughout *La Chinoise* the fundamental dilemmas in acting upon revolutionary consciousness are probed: recourse to violence; the issue of solidarity; the question of accommodating revolutionary commitment to the actual nature of contemporary culture; the matter, too, of just what constitutes revolutionary art. In their cottage, sealed off from the outside world, the students fill the walls with slogans. They fill their hearts and minds with revolutionary ethos, and attempt to create that moment of collective epiphany in which the magic electricity of genuine solidarity is summoned forth and realized.

They fail, of course. Their failure, however, is portrayed with empathy and with enthusiasm for the undertaking itself. Since the coming of the New Left, revolutionary consciousness is the province of the middle classes. As Godard himself once commented in an interview, if the workers want movies they can make their own!

All this, however, is highly problematic. The replacing of proletarian strivings for justice with middle-class yearnings for satisfaction threatens all cultural initiative on the left. Thus, a portrayal of the revolutionary ethos as boring and conventional also comes from France in the mid-1960s.

It is Georges Perec's wry and constrained novel *Les Choses (The Things: A Story of the Sixties)*. Its language is direct and informational, full of nouns and relatively uncluttered by adjectives. Its images are things; its world is a world composed of things. The characters, a couple named Jerome and Sylvia, wander through the contemporary environment of Paris, wanting the better things, the finer things, the tasteful things of life, never truly aligning these desires with their leftist politics. Theirs is a kind of sleepwalking, evoking the imagery of detached, ambling wandering as the definitive condition of modern life in the industrialized West. This imagery extends from the surrealist Breton's cry for "sleeping logicians and sleeping philosophers" to Adolf Hitler's proclamation that he moved forth in international politics with the assurance of a sleepwalker to the North American novelist Walker Percy's portrayal of the alienated and detached observer, bordering always on the edge of hypnosis or somnabulism, in *The Moviegoer*.

The characters of *The Things* have absorbed their Marxism as one conventionality among many. They accept a life slightly out of skew with the bourgeois mainstream, but that acceptance is transitory. They will seek teaching posts abroad, in the "Third World," so long as they may return to that world to which they are, after all, the rightful heirs. They will finally take reasonable, and upwardly mobile, posts in advertising in the provinces, where they can make a career and handsome incomes. The dialectic between them is destroyed. Their pairing is complete—a sterile symbiosis.

This is a new naturalism, not in the sympathetic tones and empirical style of the late-nineteenth-century's accretion of miserable detail. It is rather the unimpassioned and rote acceptance that portrays revolutionary consciousness as no longer a calling but simply a posture. Given this, is it any wonder that Western Europe has seen the random terrorism of Baader-Meinhof—a kind of anarcho-leftist *Bonnie and Clyde*—or of the Red Brigade, with its swashbuckling kidnappings and kneecappings. In Western Europe and the British Isles, the most genuine revolutionary force had become, by the 1970s, the Irish Republican Army—full of élan, commitment, and sacrifice.

The phenomenon of a reasonably affluent and leisurely Western European youth embracing the left and then progressively easing off the embrace as years go by is not so simple as it seems—not so simple, for example, as the remark once attributed to Winston Churchill would have it: "If at twenty you are not a Communist, you have no heart; if at forty you are still one, you have no head." The Left in Western Europe demonstrates enormous vitality and resiliency. Its pervasiveness in some quarters as a dimension of consciousness is quite genuinely incomprehensible to the average citizen of the United States, who does not live in an intellectual environment in which awareness is so politicized, and in which politics—if this odd phrase be permitted—are so absorbed into and recognizable as a component of consciousness itself. It is, after all, the political culture in the United States that seems world-weary, de-ideologized, and used up.

This is hardly the case, by comparison, with almost all of Western Europe.

The evidence seems to point toward most of Western Europe's evolving successfully toward greater economic justice and equality, manifesting democracy not just as a juridical, but also as a social, value. If, in the rise of this aspect of consciousness, the revolutionary ethos has appeared to moderate, this is not disastrous. Indications that the revolutionary ethos and mythos are becoming routine points not necessarily to their erosion, but rather, perhaps, to their relative success.

Chapter Four
Reactionary Consciousness

REACTIONARY CONSCIOUSNESS is a salient and significant aspect of modern and contemporary experience. Like both individual and revolutionary consciousness it is a consequent and meaningful response to aspects of modernization.

This mode of awareness, however, is most difficult to discuss constructively. It is correctly seen as the basis for the destructive movements of the Right—fascism and national socialism. Reactionary consciousness and those actions or movements based upon it are steeped in anti-intellectualism and in the embrace of irrationalism. Hence, discussion of this mode of consciousness is invariably problematic. Often the easiest choice seems to be to dismiss reactionary consciousness as a pathology, rather than to analyze it.

Reactionary consciousness differs from what may be called simply conservative consciousness. The distinction is parallel to the one that may be drawn between revolutionary and progressive modes of awareness. In its atavism, reactionary consciousness refers to elements of human nature that are ostensibly prehistorical. Individual consciousness may be assumed to have evolved along a continuum. For the Western world it proceeds from the Greeks and gains a strong orientation toward its present state during the Renaissance. In modern and contemporary life revolutionary consciousness is regarded as having evolved historically. This revolutionary consciousness is the harnessing of the rebelliousness in humans to specific ends determined by the course of history and by materialist necessity. Likewise, individual consciousness is the directing of certain traits of personality into ever more clearly defined manifestations of ego. Reactionary consciousness is, by contrast, de-evolutionary. It draws upon the past, but it does not trace a progressive continuum down the centuries toward a desired state of present being. Rather, it evokes the lost characteristics of human experience, which are collectivistic, ritualistic, and primal.

Jean-Jacques Rousseau's substitution of "general will" for individualism in the mid-eighteenth century may be regarded as a seminal expression of what developed into reactionary consciousness. Rousseau himself was no reactionary; his emphasis on the spiritual quality of awareness that binds people together may be seen, however, as such.

Implicit in the notion of a general will is the concept of community. The pursuit of community is, in turn, one of the outstanding emotional issues for modern and contemporary Western societies. This pursuit ranks alongside the struggle to determine standards for measuring superiority (and for asserting the claims based upon such measurement). It is a side (the underside, some would claim) of the quest for identity that is itself so enormously important in industrialized mass societies. The reactionary consciousness traces, to some degree, the pursuit of tradition, continuity, and connectedness. This became evident in certain instances of that complex movement that sometimes responded in a reactionary mode to certain elements of modernization, namely, Romanticism.

At the watershed in providing exploration of what community means in terms of consciousness stands, once more, Georg Friedrich Hegel. Once more, indeed, for Hegel is a reasonable point of reference in accounting for seminal expressions of the other two dimensions of modern consciousness—both individual and revolutionary. Hegel was convinced of the rationality that is present in that process that we call history. Hence he claimed right to be on the side of history. That is, what has come to be is justified in and of itself. This justification is necessary and inherent. From this perspective, the state as it emerges in its modern form may be considered as a repository of the historic will of the community. This brand of conservatism leans toward a distinctively modern mode of reactionary consciousness. The will of the people resides not only in the shared opinion of those alive at the time, but exists across time in the long-standing sentiments of the community as well. The concept of citizenry is here subordinate to the organicist notion of the "folk." The folkish definition of community is nonjuridicial and nonlegalistic. It is organicist and, if one likes (though the term is technically incorrect), racist. Reactionary consciousness marks an emotional and psychological quest for an atavistic escape from numerous facets of modernization. Reactionary consciousness is, then, another mode of rebelliousness. It may even be said that it is a particular mode in which rebellion is of the spirit; in which, in other words, rebellion is metaphysical. This metaphysical quality of reactionary rebellion distinguishes it from the rebelliousness of the Left. For the rebellion that is born of revolutionary consciousness is essentially materialistic, even though its intentions may be abstract (such as justice). Reactionary consciousness is a state of awareness that is in rebellion against the loss of community, the loss of identity, and the loss of a sense of transcendence. Reactionary consciousness rebels against loneliness and anomie, against rationalism and materialism, and against the artifices of human progress and technology. In seeking to ameliorate the condition of spiritual and emotional impoverishment brought on by modern life in industrial societies, reactionary consciousness marks an atavistic flight from nearly any aspect of experience that may be called modern. In this flight, the pursuit of a return to nature, or the embrace of instinct over reason, or the quest to recognize links between peoples which are racial rather than historical, are common. So are various forms of spiritualism, anti-utopianism, and elitism.

A striking and distinctive elaboration of reactionary consciousness became evident in the early 1800s in the Germanic territories. Novalis (the pen name of Friedrich von Hardenberg) and Friedrich Schleiermacher (1768–1834), for example, both expressed the yearning for the lost sense of belonging to unified Christendom. God's children had become divided among themselves, and this divisiveness was not only a cultural calamity but a source of the personalized sense of a loss of belonging as well. The shift from concerns that could be described properly as religious to ones that were ethnic and nationalistic proved easy. The quasi-religious quality of national patriotic fervor was hence given a philosophical grounding and a cultural expression.

Johann Fichte, leaning heavily on a predecessor of Novalis and Schleiermacher named Johann Herder, advanced an argument that was grounded in the linguistic distinctiveness of ethnic groups. In his addresses to the "German nation," delivered at Berlin in 1807, Fichte propounded an ardent notion of the organic links between contemporary generations and all persons of similar ethnicity who had ever lived before them. This notion opened the possibility for mythologizing history and investing a people's past with an organicist and spiritual dynamic that was passed from generation to generation through the course of centuries. Fichte had company, of course, with regard to this mode of thinking. Ludwig Jahn (1778–1852) and Ernst Arndt (1769–1860) were prominent among its adherents in the Germanic regions. Some form of it also seemed influential on Adam Mickiewicz in Poland and on Giuseppe Mazzini in Italy—both regions of ethnic culture in which a people had not succeeded in establishing a unified national state to reflect their common heritage and interests.

This mode of thinking had grown first and most notably in the German territories in reaction to the Napoleonic military conquests there. Nonetheless, it reflected a type of thinking which was paralleled elsewhere, and which might be said to be at the heart of a certain romanticized version of nationalism. This mode of reactionary consciousness received subsequent support in the nineteenth century from academic and scientific quarters, namely philology and biology. Philologists explored the origins of folktales within groups and posited theories, some of them quite fanciful, about the relationship of distinct languages to certain moral, intellectual, and political traits. In the 1850s racial theory was expounded with a vengeance, and with an obvious claim on its scientific validity, by the French Comte de Gobineau. In turn, many of the misreadings and distortions of Charles Darwin's evolutionary theory became popularized after 1860 as justifying extreme racial and ethnic distinctions and antagonisms.

In some of the so-called social interpretations of the theory of evolution, emphasis was on slogans such as "the struggle for survival," thus interpreting competition between nations as akin to the struggle for feeding grounds between animal species. The notion of adaptation of species as reflected in qualities of "fitness" of certain organisms was viewed as explaining the differences in technology and wealth between nations. Just as these views could justify competitiveness and explain inequalities between individuals, so could they the differences between races and nations.

In this instance a basis for discrimination between peoples can be biological, and measured as a function of performance. In reactionary consciousness the need to establish grounds for discrimination is prominent. The impulse toward distinctions of genius, of superiority, and of elites (although not necessarily hereditary elites) is perhaps the most characteristic quality of reactionary consciousness. These tendencies form a part of the scramble to fill a void that has become increasingly apparent with the decline of the traditional aristocracy. Throughout the nineteenth century the erosion of aristocratic domination gave rise to various modern substitutions of merit, worth, and value, which have been claimed as bases for distinguishing between individuals.

It is not without consequence that the decline of the aristocracy paralleled the rapid rise of modern nationalism. For whatever else it was, the concept of aristocracy in Europe was traditionally international. The respect demanded by aristocracy, blood ties between aristocratic lineages, and claims of domination and dynasty all transcended national boundaries, allegiances, and identities. It is also with the decline of the traditional aristocracy that the domain of "culture" itself became a bastion of distinctiveness. By mid-nineteenth century the view was clearly articulated that culture was to serve as a protection against the barbarian masses. Nearly three-quarters of a century before the frightened awareness spread that the masses were rising and ushering in a new age—a phenomenon that became widely apparent only at the time of the First World War—Matthew Arnold's essay *Culture and Anarchy* was published. In it is found a strong argument that culture must be preserved against the rise of pluralism, the erosion of standards, and the changing demands of modern society. In this instance, neither racial identity nor wealth nor strength, nor even genius, defines superiority so much as does discriminating taste.

The notion of culture itself as a chosen virtue implies the reactionary rejection of equality, yet on a different basis from the grounds on which equality may be rejected in other instances. There is an expression of hope in Matthew Arnold, and others who share his point of view, that somehow greater numbers of people can be stung into recognition of the high stakes at risk if greater numbers do not elect to preserve culture. Yet this hope is often meager, and even where it is abundant it is highly problematic. It is a dilemma that colors the thought of many sensitive observers, who wish to maintain standards of excellence on the one hand, while recognizing the desire for fairness and justice on the other. Nearly a century after Arnold, the Spanish essayist José Ortega y Gasset took on this dilemma in a broadly conceived work entitled *The Revolt of the Masses* (1930). Ortega argued that being "mass man" is a qualitative characteristic found primarily not in the proletariat but rather in certain elements of the middle class after the First World War; elements that claimed domination and sovereignty within society without accepting the responsibilities necessitated by such claims. In particular, it is the notion of community that is distorted by the point of view expressed in the "mass mentality." Whereas community had traditionally meant consciousness of individuality insofar as one is distinct in relationship to others, community in the age of the masses means merely the desire of an identifiable group to hold material advantage over some other group. Ortega sought to reaffirm humanism much as Arnold sought more broadly to reaffirm culture, as a way of distinguishing a sensibility that marks off the human from a merely quantitative natural order.

Neither Arnold nor Ortega endorsed Nietzsche's notion that all superior cultures must perforce be based upon cruelty. Yet both shared with Nietzsche (as do a number of other thinkers and artists) the call for a recognition of superiority. In the modern context this normally falls short of a call for the ascendancy and reign of a class of "philosopher kings." When Nietzsche speaks of the Übermensch, he is after all referring to an individual whose superiority is of the intellect and forged in dedication to the life of the mind. Here there is no sense of the Übermensch coercing others. The Nietzschean hero is a loner who can do without disciples. Hence, Nietzsche's views reflect a mode of individual consciousness, and only by extension are they to be classed with reactionary consciousness proper.

After the failed nationalist rebellions of 1848, which were dominated by romanticist myth and yearning, nationalism itself changed extensively. The simplest historical discription of that change notes a transition of nationalism from radical or revolutionary political effect before 1848 to conservative effect after that date. Here, however, the interest is not in the fact that conservative elements in most of industrialized Europe harnessed nationalism soon after 1850. Nor is our concern with the fact that after Italy and Germany were unified in 1871, the movements of national self-determination that drew attention were outside Europe's heartland—either among the Eastern European peoples or the Irish. We focus rather on the acceleration in the awareness of the human being as defined in identification with the nation, and with the spirit manifested in the nation's traditions and history. These forms of identification became dominant in all the industrial nations, in all elements within society, and across all ages and classes. As a phenomenon they spread too rapidly and thoroughly to be accounted for simplistically.

Nationalism can be viewed, of course, as an element of "false consciousness" fostered and manipulated by political and economic elites who latch on to its appeal as a way of managing increasingly complex modern societies. The fact of such manipulation, in a great many instances at least, seems unarguable. That fact, however, does not account entirely for the original appeal of this mode of consciousness. Nationalism, it appears, is a viable substitute for an eroded and lost sense of community. This aspect of its function is compensatory. In a modern world in which dislocation, discrimination, rupture, separation, and discontinuity are seen as increasingly overwhelming characteristics of experience, it is the felt loss of community—and with that loss all the assumptions about it—that needs be recaptured. Nationalism provides such a vehicle of recapture. Its notions are no more compelling intellectually than the leftist consciousness of a class solidarity that is international, transcending all national boundaries. Moreover, it is no more appealing than the notion of the Christian oneness of Europe, as advanced in modern times by romantics such Novalis, de Maistre, and Coleridge. From 1850 to 1945, however, nationalist awareness was ascendant and dominant in the European heartland (and, for that matter, in all the Western world). Complex and convoluted explanations may be offered as to why this was so. A simple interpretation would have it that national identity is simply more concrete, or less abstract, than class solidarity.

Moreover, class solidarity is subject to erosion through cooptation and social mobility, both of which are features of modern experience. Nationalism can be identified presumably with immutable characteristics, insofar as ethnicity can become racialized and given a scientific basis, as was the case after the 1860s. Nationalism can be considered as the dominant quality in culture as well, so long as the means of expression in a culture are representational and linear, and writing is in a vernacular national language. The watershed of national consciousness as a specific mode of reactionary consciousness was at its apogee between 1870 and the First World War. This was also the period in which the culture of the European heartland was at its peak as representational, linear, and written. After the First World War, the challenges to the assumptions upon which this culture was based became rife. Nationalism became a wild passion unleashed between the two wars, especially in Italy and Germany, but elsewhere as well, including the Stalinist Soviet Union.

Among thinkers and artists in Europe after 1870, nationalism became a common passion: common, though not quite universal. Nietzsche was no nationalist, although ironically his particular antidote to egalitarianism and democratization would later be drawn upon by the most rabid and extreme of national groups—the Nazis in Germany. The Left, of course, maintained its ostensibly unflinching commitment to internationalism and hence its attack upon nationalism as the tawdriest mode of false consciousness. The Left promoted internationalism with a vengeance at the turn of the century and right before the First World War. Yet that promoting often led to nationalist struggles within the ranks of the Left itself. In any case, the Left was not in the ascendant, either intellectually or culturally, at the time. In sum, the permeation of public consciousness by nationalism escaped the direct frontal attack of most thinkers before the First World War. It is difficult to find evidence that nationalism, even where it was attacked, was regarded as anything more than a seductive panacea for both the bourgeois philistines and the unwashed proletariat masses. In the late 1920s, however, the iconoclastic French free-thinker Julien Benda published a germane essay entitled *The Betrayal of the Intellectuals*. Benda traced what he called the sell-out of Western intellectuals back to the year 1870 and to the source of their sell-out: their embrace of nationalism. Benda posited the notion of the nationalization of the Western mind-set; it was precisely among those who Benda believed should have been counted on to resist it that nationalism flourished, thus undermining the traditional vocation of the intellectual as Benda saw it. That vocation was a commitment to a dispassionate quest for the truth, a project that could be carried out only in a frame of mind that accepted the intellectual's role—criticism of all worldly credos and causes as against any temptation to advocate for one or another of them.

In general, Benda condemned that quality of the modern mind that fails to understand that many values, such as equality, exist only in the abstract. In this regard his thinking may be labeled reactionary. Toward the central impulse of reactionary consciousness in his own age, however, Benda was hostile. That hostility toward nationalism was directed primarily toward thinkers and artists identifiable on the political Right, such as Treitschke in Germany, D'Annuncio in Italy, and Péguy and Barrès in France.

The mentality and point of view that Benda attacked with such vigor is manifested well in the fiction of Maurice Barrès. *The Uprooted* (1897) inaugurates a trilogy published by Barrès as "The Novel of National Energy." That general title itself marks the consciousness of national identification as not merely historical. Rather, it is a force that is vital, charged, natural, and psychological: such, at least, is a satisfactory superficial description of what the choice of the word "energy" means in this context.

A central character of Barrès's novel is Boutellier, an instructor at an academic preparatory school. Boutellier is a free-thinker, a man of liberated mind and liberating spirit, who sets the quest for truth above all practicality and all partisan passions. Such a character precisely embodies those qualities which Benda would attribute to an intellectual who remains loyal to his calling. Yet the fictional Boutellier of the novel is destructive. His free-thinking points toward the mentality of resentment, the breaking of rules, and the uprooting of institutions so that their validity and purpose within the national culture are brought under attack. The students who follow Boutellier's thinking are led down a path of disillusionment and uprootedness. They are not taught tradition, but rather they are schooled in a carping and resentful criticism of it. Such students have gone "modern" with a vengeance, in just that manner which is to the reactionary consciousness so contemptible. Their individualism leads toward a detaching of ego-consciousness from the priorities of the community and of the race. They fall prey to the barbarism of the modern world, which is the soulless measuring of success in terms not of aligning one's spirit to the nation's but simply of personal gratification.

Boutellier's students are being raised as rule breakers. His progressivism imparts to them only the basis for the erosion of standards, shared values, and legitimate sovereignty and authority. The complaint against Boutellier's influence is the cry against that which in modern and contemporary society is so common. That commonality is the breaking of strictures and the exercise of self-indulgence and of narcissistic egoism. This is the barbarism decried by traditionalists: the demand for equality and independence without recognition of the responsibilities thereby implied. Boutellier shows not an iota of understanding of the necessity to temper individual impulses in favor of national cultural values and historically derived and received collective values.

The Uprooted portrays several interrelated themes of reactionary consciousness. Saint-Philn, the student from Lorraine, reflects that strain of provincial regionalism that is part of the national French spirit. Alsace-Lorraine was from 1871 to 1919 annexed to Germany, indicating at the surface level the unquestionable revanchist theme in the novel for the territory's repatriation to France.

The plot is complicated also by an intrigue resulting in the murder of a young Oriental woman. She is the former mistress of one of the students and the victim of two others. The significance of this incident, however, is manifest in the implication drawn from it, specifically that the pursuit of true equality is a sham, because the notion of equality is based upon the false assumption that individuals of different background can somehow overcome precisely what it is that they are. For race and ethnicity are immutable aspects of personality.

Ideas of racial and ethnic identity, which are modes of consciousness, were perhaps at their peak in the Western world at the turn of the century. Imperialism fed racism and also fed off it. Nationalism wallowed in the semantic confusion of ethnicity with race (in the late nineteenth century talk of the "German race" or the "French race" went on in all sorts of quarters, including scholarly ones). As the certitude of social role and status eroded, racial and ethnic differences became definitive of distinctions that were claimed to be permanent and unalterable.

This semantic confusion—this mode of consciousness that identified human quality with nationality and meaning and value with national tradition—was at the core of the European crisis in the first half of the twentieth century. The crisis reached fever pitch with Hitler and the National Socialists in Germany, who rose to mass strength in the late 1920s and who took power after 1933. Yet this was not strictly a German malady: it was a European disease that ate away at all areas of thought and culture. It visibly permeated European politics and diplomacy. Less obviously, it dominated a significant terrain in the collective consciousness.

It was this nationalistic mode of reactionary consciousness that dominated the most ferocious and historically telling development in Western history during the first half of the century—the rise and short-lived triumph of nazism. This murderous movement and the episode of destruction that it unleashed can be comprehended as drawing together numerous strands of reactionary consciousness and absorbing them into a vital and aggressive force by dint of the fundamental appeal to national awareness as primarily racial.

In Hans Grimm's novel *Folk without Space* (1926), the aspect of consciousness linked to the geopolitics of nationalism is manifest. This is an instance, however, in which the idea-in-consciousness lies beyond its embodiment in a work of narrative fiction. The Nazi movement itself and its leader, Adolf Hitler, enacted the mode of national consciousness in its fullest. In Nazi regalia and ritual, or in the element of performance that is obvious in Nazi rite, the reactionary mode of awareness was evident. Nowhere in any work of art enacting a mode of consciousness is national consciousness as intense as it was in Hitler's own enactment of it. When, for example, during the Nuremberg party rally of 1934 Hitler speaks simply of Germany, that mode of awareness was evoked. Captured for posterity in the film *Triumph of the Will* (directed by Leni Riefenstahl), Hitler crosses his arms upon his chest in priestly fashion, looks heavenward, and intones simply the words: "Germany; Germany; Germany!" This is a manifestation of the pinnacle of national consciousness. The moment is mystical, and redolent with both meaning and value. It encapsulates the rush of consciousness toward the atavistic irrationality that links a human soul with racial ancestors through blood-ties and with the soil itself of the national homeland.

It is the mode of reactionary consciousness, of which this atavistic and mysticized nationalism is a part, that was the basis for Hitler's program of national aggrandizement and his call for German hegemony on the continent. At the same time, the dominant strain of awareness in German national socialism was ethnic and racial. Thus, nazism was an ideology that could not be exported effectively to other peoples and other places. It compromised severely any prospect for acceptance of the "New Order" imposed on the foreign territories occupied by German armies between 1939 and 1944.

It was the heightened realization of this particular mode of reactionary consciousness that also rendered Nazi anti-Semitism so unrelenting and murderous. This was an anti-Semitism that modernized the phenomenon of opposition to the Jew, while at the same time manifesting a rationale for it that was unabashedly antimodern. In this modernizing of traditional European anti-Semitism, biological and racial contempt replaced religious antagonism. The Jews' crime was not their rejection of Christ as saviour, but rather their having short-circuited the authentic and natural pattern of historical development to which all other peoples have been subject. The Jews, according to this interpretation of their history in the diaspora, had not engaged—as an ethnic community—in the struggle for survival that is geared strictly to the competition among national groups for sovereignty over feeding grounds. The Jews had cheated both history and biological necessity. This allegation amounts to a heightening of the culpability of their legendary trickery. Like parasites, the Jews had come into the ethnic national communities of other peoples and fed off them.

It is not difficult to see how this convoluted reasoning connected with so many of the standardized images of anti-Semitism. Nor is it difficult to comprehend that in an age in which national consciousness swept over the European heartland, from 1870 to 1945, suspicion about Jews should rise. For one of the consistent facts about Jews in modern times is that national allegiance on the part of any Jew has been suspect. Since Jews have been considered to be of a unique racial or ethnic stock they cannot be accepted in full authenticity as "truly" English, French, German, or Italian.

Only with the rise of national consciousness to the forefront of reactionary awareness, accompanied by the rising secularization of Western society, did anti-Semitism diverge from its historic course of nearly a thousand years of exclusively religious antagonism. In one sense at least, it is more pernicious in its modern form. Biological and racial anti-Semitism offers no exit. Religious anti-Semitism had always provided, minimally at least, the possibility (as reprehensible as it may have been) of conversion. The acceptance of baptism, or the repression into secrecy of Jewish rite and ritual, could normally accommodate the consistently hostile demands of the Christian majority. Once anti-Semitism became based on blood or race, and once these categories were established as a central mode of reactionary consciousness, the murder of Jews from 1941 to 1945 became comprehensible (though still irrational). Thus, modern anti-Semitism is interrelated with the phenomenon of modern national consciousness.

Modern national consciousness is a source of identity. It provides a focus for the psychic energy of groups. It is a repository for aggressive impulses, hatreds, and antagonism; in sum, however, it is primarily a refuge from freedom. Sociologically, it is a phenomenon that after 1870 existed and flourished on the basis of its deep roots in envy. That envy arose grudgingly and in contempt for the Jewish capacity to maintain their own group identity and awareness against the onslaught of modernization. In fact, the Jewish sense of identity and of community not only survived the challenges of modernization but prospered over against them. In the European heartland during the nineteenth century Jews were the beneficiaries of various aspects of modernization. The legislative reforms of the Napoleonic era in regard to civil liberties for Jews were nowhere completely rescinded by the forces of restoration and reaction after 1815. With the rise of commerce, industry, cities, and a society in which mobility through educational advancement and entrepreneurial achievement flourished, the social and economic status of Jews improved. Claims by critics that the Jews became dominant in certain fields were exaggerated, as were the estimates of Jewish wealth and status. It was not, however, any statistically measurable accomplishment by Jews on which anti-Semitism was based.

The underside of the processes of modernization consisted of feelings and perceptions of dislocation, uprootedness, and home-lessness. These were forms of alienation, related directly to the erosion of familial bonds and of the positive values and reinforcements of community. Such deterioration may not have been measured statis-tically, either. Nonetheless, perception of it—whether verifiable or not—was widely felt. Again, the Jews appeared to be circumventing the wages of modern progress, just as through history they had eluded the necessity of struggling as a nation for feeding ground. That the horrors of deprivation and alienation were present and had their toll upon the Jews of Europe as a collectivity is evident. The instances of accomplishments by Jews in the arts and in formal thought bear witness to the penchant of many Jews to master "mod-ernism," based on some old Jewish specialties—dislocation, uproot-edness, and homelessness. Hence over the worst ravages of mod-ernization, Jews appeared to triumph. That victory, which evoked the resentment of others, was documented in Emile Durkheim's classic masterpiece of early sociology on suicide (1896). Tracing the act of suicide primarily to the feeling of anomie, Durkheim's statistics meas-ured a suicide rate for Jews in Europe that was infinitesimal.

The enactment of anti-Semitism in the work of art is itself subsidiary to the more dominant strain of consciousness enacted as nationalist awareness. Yet if there is one work in which anti-Semitism was tied to national consciousness adequately it is perhaps the 1940 film produced in Germany and directed by Veit Harland, *The Jew Suess*. This is an adaptation of a novel by the Jewish author Lion Feucht-wanger, first published in 1925. It was also, as the film historian David Stewart Hull has noted, not the first filmed version of the work. In 1932 a version was produced in Great Britain. Clearly, its thematic material and characterizations appealed well beyond the German audience.

In the 1940 film version, the narrative portrays the conniving and power-thirsty machinations of a Jew named Suess Oppenheimer. In service to the duchy of Wuerttemberg, Suess engages in financial wizardry and chicanery to underwrite the duke's debaucheries while paving his own path to power. As a story of financial intrigue and of aristocratic excesses, the action is slow-paced. Two scenes in the film, however, are both central and dramatically potent. Suess abducts the young blonde Dorothea Sturm and rapes her. The scene evinces a full command of the most important and distinctive artistic characteristic of film-making—editing. The shots of the mustachioed, oily-headed Jew forcing himself upon Dorothea are intercut with scenes of Dorothea's young, patriotic boyfriend being tortured. The Jew's rape of his young victim is connected visually with the imprisonment and restraint of the young man who personifies Germanic righteousness and patriotism. Dorothea drowns herself in shame and horror after Oppenheimer is done with her. The exploitation of this act of despoiling is telling. It has its parallel in another film produced in Germany several years earlier, *Frisians in Peril* (1935). In it the plight of a community of ethnic Germans in Russia at the time of the Bolshevik revolution is portrayed. A young German woman who has betrayed her blood lineage by sleeping with a Russian commits suicide out of guilt and shame.

The intertwining of the notion of racial purity with sexuality and violence is revealing. Both instances which have been referred to here suggest the deep psychological roots of racial and ethnic antagonism. In the modern age these antagonisms have been made most active—and have been exploited most successfully, under the banner of nationalism. At its apogee, nationalism is of such force and appeal that apparently a good deal of that human energy normally labeled "libidinal" can be invested in it. Nationalism can become in the mind's eye a be-all and do-all. The nation can be raised to the level of godhead or placed on the plane of love object. The nation can function in consciousness as saviour, lover, mother, or father.

It was in national socialism that reactionary consciousness, and the nationalist aspect of that consciousness, reached a crescendo of violence and passion. Fascism in Italy and falangism in Spain are often considered to be movements made of the same ideological and emotional stuff as nazism, but they are not. Whereas they are essentially movements which can be understood in light of tradition and as being to some degree intent on preservation of privilege for the established orders, nazism is another matter. Too complex to be treated in detail here, the Nazi phenomenon can be called nonetheless a nearly full-fledged embrace of reactionary consciousness. In its atavism, its invocation of mythology, its incarnation of Hitler-as-Messiah, its murderous anti-Semitism, its antimodern calls for a return to the soil, or its equally antimodern attack upon avant-garde and abstract art, nazism mobilized reactionary consciousness. Hence its impact as a movement, its means and its style, look for all the world as if they were revolutionary, while the content of the movement remained unabashedly reactionary.

Yet Hitler and the Nazis were, as the British historian A. J. P. Taylor put it, "the end product of a civilization of clever talk." The reactionary consciousness that they forged into frenzied action abounded elsewhere in Europe, in various quarters, across different classes and levels of society. The nationalism, the anti-Semitism, the antimodernism, the contempt for and fear of democratization—all these were elements of that consciousness. That consciousness was to be taken literally, invested with enormous collective energy, and acted out with ferocity in Germany after 1933.

As an aspect of consciousness the particular elaboration called nationalism prevailed in Europe just prior to the Second World War in every class and stratum of society. In a film entitled *The Grand Illusion*, produced in France in 1937 and directed by Jean Renoir, this element is manifest. This manifestation is unlikely, since the film's director had since 1936 identified himself and his art increasingly with the leftist popular front government of Léon Blum in France. It is quite possible that the presence of a nationalistic core in the film came to be there over and against the conscious intentions of the film's creators.

The social historian Pierre Sorlin, in particular, has pointed out the thematic ambiguity of *The Grand Illusion*; he has clarified the elements of national sentiment that quite paradoxically permeate the movie. Here, in passing, it might be noted that the motion picture is characteristically a more ambiguous form of expression than the novel or the theatrical play. Since movies are composed of visual images, which are concrete rather than abstract, it is likely that the economics of the cinema have rendered the content of movies particularly ambiguous. That ambiguity, which opens the range of interpretations on the part of individual viewers, translates commercially into an increased potential audience for any film.

The Grand Illusion is set during the First World War. The narrative begins when two French aviators are captured by the Germans. Maréchal is of humble background; Boieldieu is of aristocratic lineage. In prison they are joined by a French Jew, Lieutenant Rosenthal, whose parents are wealthy. The action centers on their relationship, compounded by the presence of the German commandant of the fortress where they are finally incarcerated, Major von Raufenstein.

Raufenstein befriends Boieldieu. Their exchanges portray the sense of honor, dignity, and Anglomania that the aristocrats had traditionally maintained across national boundaries. Theirs is a world not only in retreat, but crashing to its end. Raufenstein's pursuit of the myth of aristocratic unity combines arrogance and pathos. In the dramatic turning point of the film it is Boieldieu's ruse that permits Maréchal and Rosenthal to escape together while he creates a diversion for them. His antics cause Raufenstein to have to shoot him, hence sealing the imagery of the aristocracy's self-destruction.

Yet throughout the film it is clear that Boieldieu is always a Frenchman first. The aristocratic myth is Raufenstein's exclusively. His characterization may be considered that of a man of honor; yet a deeper look into the portrayal reveals that he is dogged, unyielding, disciplined, and deluded. The negative German stereotypes finally abound here, even when indications of a sympathetic portrayal are present. A young German war widow takes in Maréchal and Rosenthal at her farmhouse. Sympathetic as she is, she falls for the non-Jew, and she and Maréchal quickly become lovers. However, when Rosenthal recovers from his injuries, he and Maréchal flee to Switzerland.

Grand Illusion may contain pacifist suggestions. Its mentality, however, is nationalist rather than internationalist. French individualism and resourcefulness are here at the fore. The German enemy, and even the British and Russian allies, are stereotyped negatively. The action vindicates French national unity based on idealized mutual sacrifice and classless solidarity. Moreover, while the film steers clear of overt anti-Semitism (except when Maréchal calls Rosenthal a "dirty Jew" after their escape), Rosenthal's character bears many of the stereotypes out of which an anti-Semitic caricature may be made.

The consciousness enacted in *Grand Illusion* is reactionary. Whether it might be translated into justification for behavior that is not reactionary is a separate matter. Consciousness and action are not simply interchangeable, and the latter never follows directly from the former. A modification in the ascendancy of national consciousness occurs in the European heartland with the end of the Second World War. This transformation may be seen manifest in the movie *Open City*, made by Roberto Rossellini in Rome just as the German occupation of the city was ending.

The movie presents negative stereotypes of its German characters, except perhaps for the officer Hartmann, who drunkenly comes clean in his own words of the German crimes. Yet these stereotypes are anchored relatively firmly in the historical record. Given the moment of the film's production, which was right at the end of the German occupation, the portrayals are remarkably mild. *Open City* gives the appearance of addressing Italian national rebirth; it deals primarily with the exploits of patriotic partisans. There is a wrinkle in this, however. The Italian national past and heritage are hardly elevated. Italian Fascists are portrayed no more kindly than the Germans, although the absence of many Italian Fascists can be seen as suggesting a whitewash of national responsibility for the scourge of right-wing authoritarianism. Most importantly, the Italian resistance is portrayed through two characters, the priest Don Pietro and the Communist party functionary Manfredi. Resistance is carried on by two individuals who, each in his own way, represent international bodies—the Catholic church and the international Communist movement, respectively.

Open City, too, may be thought of as ambiguous. That ambiguity, however, is perhaps here most positively understood as genuine tentativeness. Both Don Pietro and Manfredi—who have direct contact with each other only fleetingly once, but whose fates are intertwined—die at the hands of the Germans. Their antifascism has brought them together. Their deaths leave the young boys to walk off in unison, whistling, from the site of Don Pietro's execution, back toward the city, which may be seen in the distance. The tenuous relationship between Don Pietro and Manfredi is, in fact, the hope held out for the future: that is, that the intellectual, emotional, and psychological power of the two forces they represent, namely catholicism and the political Left, can absorb national consciousness through their transcendence of it.

Throughout the heartland of Europe, that future has since become the recent past and the present. To a great extent, national consciousness has eroded. The frenzied excesses of Hitler and the Nazis (along with Mussolini and the Fascists) threw nationalism, and those aspects of consciousness on which it was based, into disrepute. The European disease of nationalism, if not cured, is at least in remission. Awareness is growing of a perspective on collective experience that is European rather than national, as the formal organs of West European unity (the Common Market, the European Parliament, Euratom, the Western European Union, NATO), develop. De Gaulle's highly successful political career after 1958 may have appeared to be based in the old, nationalistic chauvinism that regarded France as the grand nation of God's own design, but appearances deceive. Even de Gaulle had to posture as a "European" foremost, promoting France as leading Europe's revitalization of a third force that opposed

both the superpowers. Moreover, for all the evidence of obstruc-
tionism on the part of the French representatives to the European
Economic Community and other Western European bodies, it remains
arguable whether the population still widely shares in the nationalistic
mode of reactionary consciousness.

On the score of nationalist feeling, there is a split in consciousness
that is generational. Persons born after 1940 in Europe do not
necessarily measure collective experience and assess group values in
nationalistic terms. Nowhere is this clearer than in the German Federal
Republic, where the evidence points dramatically to increasing acceptance of Germany's post-1945 division on the part of people born
since 1940. For the older generation of Germans, especially those
born before 1920, the loss of German unification and the lingering
desire to somehow right that wrong persists in various measures. A
substantial role in the generational tension that has existed in Western
Europe since the early 1960s is played by division on the issue of
nationalism. Age (for Western Europe) and geography (if all of Europe
is considered) are the primary determinants of nationalistic sentiment.
Nationalism is still a meaningful repository of collective value and
sentiment among the ethnic groups in Eastern Europe, although such
is not the case outside the Communist block. Hungarian nationalism
(1956), Czechoslovakian nationalism (1968), and Polish nationalism
(1981) have been at the center of resistance to Soviet domination
exercised through the aegis of national Communist parties loyal to
Moscow. In Western Europe protest and political activism bear no
similar trace of being offshoots of frustrated residual national consciousness.

The Western European resentment toward elements of economic,
political, and cultural influence which have been exerted there by
the United States since 1945 goes well beyond being rooted in national
consciousness. National identity is no longer even a necessary point
of departure in the articulation of that resentment. In the form of
representational expression that has been dominant since 1945, namely
the motion picture, a pattern of attempting to mediate thematically
the West European-U.S. relationship has been evident. This pattern
begins, perhaps, with Rossellini's celebration of the liberation of Italy
at war's end, in quasidocumentary style and with generally sympathetic imagination, in *Paisan* (1945). The theme continues into the
decade of the 1980s with Alain Resnais's film *My American Uncle*
(1980). In Resnais's film the complex web of disjointed narrative and
commentary suggests on the one hand the social and economic

injustice of the United States: the movie ends with scenes of the abandoned buildings and gutted facades of the South Bronx in New York, which are reminiscent of the photos and newsreel footage of European cities bombed during World War II. On the other hand, the allusion is clear that the United States still possesses mystical qualities for Western Europeans, even though it is no longer the promised land for waves of immigrants from Europe. As a character says in the film's dialogue: "America doesn't exist; I know, because I've lived there."

This mediation of the West European-U.S. relationship has occurred also in such Western European movies as the Italian "spaghetti westerns" of the 1960s, in which the legends and myths of the American West, as well as the cinematographic *coda* of Hollywood, are playfully but effectively debunked. In a more self-conscious way a number of West German films of the 1970s explore the American presence in the Western European mind and spirit. Examples include *The American Soldier* (R. W. Fassbinder, 1970); *Damn, This America* (V. Vogeler, 1973); *Alice in the Cities* (W. Wenders, 1973); *Amerika* (K. Thome, 1974); *Made in Germany and USA* (K. Thome, 1974); *Emden Goes to the USA* (K. Wildenhan, 1976); *The American Friend* (W. Wenders, 1977); and *I Often Think of Hawaii* (E. Mikesch, 1978). The explorations of relationships with the United States, its myths, and its imagery are extensive. As a character puts it in yet another West German film of the 1970s, *Kings of the Road*: "The Americans have even colonized our subconscious."

Since 1945 the shift in Western Europe is in the direction of a unified Western European consciousness. That shift is in the ascendancy, and, while not unchallenged, seems likely to continue for the near future at least. It is in clear contradistinction to the elements of national consciousness which were pushed to the extreme during the first half of the twentieth century. Even terrorism in Western Europe became transnational in the late 1960s and 1970s. The only ethnically defined cleavage that has flourished since the Second World War is that of northern European vs. the Mediterranean. This is a complex phenomenon, fraught with a number of cultural and economic issues. The legions of "guest workers" are the "new Helots" who will undertake unskilled labor and every menial task. They have been shuttling from south to north across Europe since the late 1950s. Oddly, fictional literary works portraying the special social, cultural, and psychological characteristics of this widely shared experience are surprisingly few. While a number of representational works allude to the issue, few enter its realms. Franco Brusati's movie *Bread and Chocolate* (1978), about an Italian laborer awash in the sanitized land of money and mountains—Switzerland—is an exception to that rule, as is R. W. Fassbinder's *Ali*.

Throughout all of Western Europe, national consciousness is not dead, buried, or forgotten. Its manifestations by the 1970s seem to have been few, but those few are complex and confusing. This complexity itself is portrayed well in a motion picture completed in 1977, *Our Hitler—A Film from Germany*. The movie, directed by Hans-Juergen Syberberg, is composed of four parts (with a combined running length of over seven hours). Its temporal framework is a panorama of German history from the late nineteenth century through the Nazi era. This sweep of time is embraced, however, without extension into space. The surrealistic action is confined to a darkened studio set. Documentary and newsreel footage is sparingly intercut, along with the still photographs, mannequins, and puppets portraying historical personages of the 1920s and 1930s.

The film parallels the rise of the motion picture as a form of expression with the rise of fascism. In an early episode the Mad King Ludwig of Bavaria holds forth in monologue inside of Edison's "Black Maria" (the first movie production studio). The monologue of the child murderer in the Fritz Lang film *M* (1931), who protests his inability to do other than he has done, is counterpointed against appearances of Hitler as circus ringmaster, as Frankenstein, as Charlie Chaplin, and as Nero. The Hitler everywhere is the Hitler in all of us. Scenes of the Nazis burning books are juxtaposed against scenes alluding to German film-makers in the 1920s and in the 1970s. The narrator intones the rhetorical question: "Where will this end? Hitler books beget Hitler films!"

In the second episode of the movie Hitler proclaims himself as the end product of Western civilization. The proclamation is followed by a scene of three Negro GIs dancing with a blond woman at Richard Wagner's tombstone. Later a ventriloquist's dummy Hitler explains that, having failed at art, he turned to politics. That turn, he boasts, has changed many things—now the Russians are on the Elba River, the Jews have their own state, and the United States has a new colony. In that regard, "Consider where the great new market of Hollywood lies."

In its imagery and in its themes, the Hitler film traverses back and forth between triviality and the level of world historical import, from scenes of a little girl holding a dog with a Hitler face to scenes of Jews being murdered in extermination camps. In the final sequences of the last episode the narrator, however, accuses Hitler himself of the trivialization of all the old German values.

The film explores the break with the past, with history, with culture, and with tradition that is characteristic of the European experience since 1945. In this particular work, which is heavily permeated with self-conscious pursuit of a lost quality of German essence, the context appears to be specifically German. Beyond this, however, may be perceived an atavistic, reactionary core, which transcends the particular Germanic context. Specifically, the undisguised resentment toward the United States and its cultural forms (especially the Hollywood movie) reflects aspects of a repressed or frustrated national consciousness. Hence, the United States is resented in the 1970s and 1980s in the European heartland not simply by leftists who oppose her mercenary capitalist imperialism, but by those who rebel against the Americanization of culture, which ostensibly destroys the rootedness of culture in historic national sources. In numerous instances, anti-Americanism may be understood as being anchored in nationalistic atavism. The anti-American posture provides, indeed, an excellent disguise for passions that have been discredited in their own right. Given the ideological situation in Western Europe in the 1960s and 1970s, it is also quite possible for leftist anti-Americanism and atavistic nationalistic anti-Americanism to coexist—not only in the same communities, but in the same individuals as well.

Nationalistic atavism is a mode of reactionary consciousness that is suspect. It bases reaction in the notion that the nation state (a modern institution) manifests a tribalism and a return to "natural" social relations. Compared to more thorough-going modes of reactionary consciousness, nationalistic atavism appears to be little more than half-hearted philistinism warped by collective conformism.

The reactionary consciousness manifested, for example, in D. H. Lawrence's *The Plumed Serpent* (1926) is quite different. Lawrence had gone outside of Europe proper, just as several works portraying revolutionary consciousness or individual consciousness did. In this instance, the novel is set in Mexico. The narrative focuses on revival of the Quetzalcoatl (or Plumed Serpent) religion. This focus is complicated by the presence of Kate, an Irishwoman of middle age, who bridges the vitalism and sadism of this religion with the rationalism of Europe. She, in fact, has journeyed to the shores of Lake Sayula in Mexico in flight from the life of modern Europe.

Don Ramon is the messianic leader of the cult that revives the ancient religion of the American continent. Here acted out is the destruction of Christ and Christianity, and in its place the ascendancy of a dictatorship over inferior beings. In Don Ramon's reversion to primitivism, to nature at its deepest heart and core, is the strength of his own ascendancy and power of will. This religiosity is a vehicle, too, for fulfilling his manhood. Here is a mode of reactionary consciousness that asserts the interrelationship of maleness and mastery. The erotic, and specifically that which is both erotic and masculine, dominates. At one point the waters of Lake Sayula become spermlike and milky. Kate gives herself to Don Ramon's disciple Don Cipriano; he, emphatically, does not give himself to her. Repeatedly, Cipriano denies sexual satisfaction to her, and this she comes to accept. She gravitates steadily away from her independent and liberated selfhood toward aquiescence and subservience. She accepts his secrecy and hence endorses his supremacy. She becomes finally like Teresa, Don Ramon's wife. She exists for him and for his desire. He exists beyond her and beyond the frustration of a consciousness that is meaningful only as an expression of a being's humanity: beyond humanity for Don Ramon is his connectedness with nature and with the cosmos.

The Plumed Serpent enacts the mythos of animism and nature, the cult of leadership, the force of violence and sacrifice, and the supremacy of the male. It manifests that extension of the romantic quest for a return to nature that dates back to the very end of the eighteenth century. It is, however, permeated by an embrace of primitivism, darkness, and irrationality that is not found in the more bucolic, pastoral, and nostalgic qualities, which partly characterized certain modes of Romanticism proper. In the cataclysm of the First World War, the last hopes for preservation of the world as it had so long been seemed to many to perish. More notably, the grudging granting of female suffrage right after the First World War (throughout Western Europe except for France and Switzerland), the altered population balance between males and females as a result of male casualties in the war, and the changed social and sexual mores that characterized the 1920s in industrialized societies marked a heightening of the fear of feminization of society. A mode of reactionary consciousness reacts clearly against this threat. The fear of sexual impotence meshes well with the perceptions of a loss of control brought on in modern times by the rise of technology, the growth of bureaucracy, and the agglomeration of population. Hence, the fear of feminization on the part of males who have dominated previously economic, social, and political life is a complex cultural and ideological formulation that originates in collective psychoerotic tension.

The Plumed Serpent is nearly didactic, and most certainly unrelenting, in both the erotic ethic and the sociopolitical program that it manifests. By comparison, the motion picture directed by Fritz Lang in 1927 in Germany, *Metropolis*, is more subtle and ambiguous. *Metropolis* portrayed, however, several of the primary modes of reactionary consciousness as they existed in Western Europe between the two world wars.

Metropolis is, first of all, an anti-Utopian portrayal of the future. In that regard it anticipates the spate of anti-Utopian novels that have appeared since the Second World War. From British writers alone, for example, one counts George Orwell's *1984*, Aldous Huxley's *Brave New World*, William Golding's *Lord of the Flies*, Rex Warner's *Aerodrome* and *The Wild Goose Chase*, and both *The Clockwork Orange* and *The Wanting Seed* by Anthony Burgess. In the futuristic world of *Metropolis*, a small clique of rulers live in the upper city and rule over the mass of slave workers, who toil in misery beneath the surface of the earth.

The dramatic action of the motion picture is triggered by the impulse of the son of the master of Metropolis, who, seeing a young woman from the worker's underworld, decides to pursue her into the depths. His initial reaction to this descent is one of horror. Impulsively, again, he takes on a worker's garb and toils at one of the machines until he is exhausted. The young woman whose innocent allure has drawn him into the depths of the workers' underground city is Maria. She is portrayed as a kind of leader among the workers. She preaches patience and holds out the hope to them that a deliverer will intervene on their behalf.

The only character in *Metropolis* who stands outside the divided world of rulers and slave workers is the magician and inventor Rotwang. The master of Metropolis, concerned about the protest movement among the workers led by Maria, enlists Rotwang to subvert her influence. Rotwang kidnaps her and substitutes for her a robot that he creates in her image. The robot, who rejects all of Maria's pacifist teachings, incites the workers to riot. They do so, wreaking pandemonium and havoc upon themselves. They destroy many of the great generators in the underground city. This causes massive flooding, and threatens them and their children. Heroically Maria and young Fredersen save them from death in the floods.

The film ends with a scene of Rotwang attempting to escape with Maria in his clutches, while the frenzied workers burn the robot Maria on a pyre. Young Fredersen pursues Rotwang to the roof of a cathedral, daringly struggles with him there, and triumphs. Rotwang is dead. The slave workers, represented by the generator room foreman, and the ruling elite, represented by the elder Fredersen, are reconciled. Young Fredersen and Maria are arm in arm, she casting a respectfully loving, admiring, and dutiful gaze upon him. He, indeed, has acted as the living medium for bringing peace and unity to society. As the final title in the film comments, "only by mediation of the heart can the head and the hands be brought together."

Metropolis is an apt work to cite as embodying the coalescence of several themes of reactionary consciousness. Society here is portrayed beyond class differences as an organism in which unity is achieved through an abrupt change of heart. Moreover, the necessary circumstance for social unity is the elimination of the outsider, in this instance the odd magician/inventor Rotwang. Direct action by the oppressed in pursuit of justice and equality is a sham (they are led into it by the robot only) and is self-destructive (they unleash flooding that threatens only their own homes and children). The messianic leader, namely he who comes down from above to offer deliverance, offers hope for the righting of wrong—even here on earth. A woman's ascendancy into the role of shaping events and altering perceptions is limited. Behind her doing so is her true nature, which is loving and supportive. Moreover, a woman's assumption of a role that is not rightly hers invites distortion of it and disaster (i.e., the destructive machinations of the robot Maria).

The decades between the two world wars marked the high point of reactionary consciousness in the Western world. The defeat of Hitler and the Nazis, the discrediting of collaborationists and right-wing fellow travelers outside Germany, and the revelations of the murder of six million Jews discredited the Right immediately after 1945. The "hour zero" was the nadir of reactionary consciousness. A saddened and stunned Western Europe surveyed the wreckage of its civilization.

The nadir of reactionary consciousness was, however, brief. For it is understandable that the excesses of the Fascist and National Socialist can be seen as an aberration of certain directions in reactionary consciousness. They represent the passion of usurpers of genuine and legitimate authority, and the vulgarization of the nostalgia for order and simplicity into bully-boy politics. Hitler and Mussolini were then barbarians who captured, somehow, the Right—distorting its high-minded purposes. In many quarters, this explanation does not register, of course. On the Left especially the assumption of the inherent culpability of the Right prevails. In this view the traditional Right, in nearly any of its guises, leads toward Hitlerism and the Holocaust.

The interpretation is plausible that between the world wars the constructive modes of reactionary consciousness had been overwhelmed by the single-minded perversion of nationalism. Attitudes, behavior, and postures rooted unabashedly in modes of reactionary consciousness did reassert themselves quickly in Western Europe after 1945. When they did so, however, the pervasive element of nationalism that had become dominant after 1870 was for the most part purged from them.

Instead, contemporary reactionary consciousness is molded in two major directions. The first of these is in that apocalyptic vision of the future (to which the present is swiftly leading us) that has already been referred to as anti-Utopian. Whereas Utopian visions may be said to date back to Plato and *The Republic*, anti-Utopianism is a modern phenomenon. Samuel Butler's *Erewhon* (1871) contains elements of anti-Utopianism, but the work stands mainly as a relatively mild and modest satire of voguish ideas. And while the Russian émigré Zamiatin's novel *We*, first published in France in 1924, may be called anti-Utopian, its vision is still easily confused with a futurist interpretation that welcomes the joys of machinery.

George Orwell's *1984*, published in 1949, enacts this anti-Utopian reactionary consciousness well. The vision in *1984* is of a society in which a monolithic consciousness industry has taken over thought, life, and spirit. Electronics and mass communications are the vehicles of thought control in this future society. "Big Brother" is watching you, hearing you, and seeing you. Indeed, this imagery of the all-intrusive government is possibly one of the most widely accepted and believed items of fiction in Western history. The fundamental appeal of this myth in fiction may itself, in fact, be atavistic and general to the human species. Something akin to it parallels the Darwinist references to the primal horde emerging with a tyrant leader.

1984 is so effective because it ties the undermining of consciousness itself to the spread of technology. Its own consciousness in the novel is antiauthoritarian, and that with a vengeance. On the other hand, it provides an extraordinarily negative image of the masses. If democratization leads in the direction of mass society, then *1984* is antidemocratic. Clearly, the novel offers no hope of humankind saving itself. The myth of revolutionary change resulting in human liberation is debunked; so is the modest liberal or progressive faith in human reason, scientific advancement, and technology.

The novel's protagonist is Winston Smith, a marginal member of the outer ring of the ruling party. He holds a post at the Ministry of Truth, primarily on the strength of his mastery of the official party jargon into which all experience is to be duly translated, "newspeak." When one day he is engaging in the solitary pursuit of making diary comments, he realizes that he does not really love "Big Brother."

Smith's rebelliousness is not focused. It takes the form of his friendship with a rebellious younger woman named Julia. Eventually he begins seeing her frequently, and they hold trysts in a room he has rented upstairs at the antique shop belonging to a friendly character named Charington. One such afternoon a booming voice interrupts them. Smith realizes that they have been observed all along. Charington, it turns out, is a secret police functionary.

Smith is tortured and brainwashed. Eventually he is broken of spirit and professes his love to "Big Brother," just as Oceania is winning a stunning military victory in Africa. Orwell's fiction can be interpreted, of course, with simple and searing equations between "Big Brother" and Stalin and between Oceania and the U.S.S.R. If it ended at that the novel would be of interest primarily as a reflection of Orwell's personal disillusionment with the orthodox Left. *1984*, however, enacts a visceral response to modernization, democratization, technology, and bureaucracy that recoils against it no matter where it may be.

In comparison to *1984*, *A Clockwork Orange* (1962) by Anthony Burgess is far more challenging and problematic. *1984* enacts, after all, the imagery of a future in which there is little doubt or ambiguity. *1984* is the anti-Utopian novel in which bleakness reigns everywhere identifiably; there are no open questions on the nature of the barbarism. *A Clockwork Orange* is different, essentially because it is predicated on questions that are not simply political and social, but religious as well. Moreover, *A Clockwork Orange* may be said to be composed of images and elements that strike closer to home for the average reader in the Western world. For *1984* presents a fictionalized totalitarianism, whereas *A Clockwork Orange* portrays a society that is more simply progressive and sterile. The dehumanization is the product of a caretaker society, one that is anchored in the same sort of liberal behaviorism that seems rampant in so much of the Western world since the early 1960s. Education and science, after all, are ostensibly the lovely golden pathways to a world of peace and prosperity.

Fifteen-year-old Alex and his pals, who are called "droogs," engage in a wide range of adolescent urban violence. Gang wars, robberies, muggings, beatings, rape, and murder compose their repertoire. Alex is distinguised from the rest of the pack by his odd and idiosyncratic passion for music, including the works of Beethoven and especially the *Ninth Symphony*.

Abandoned by the other droogs after a murder, Alex is imprisoned. There he is selected for a complete reconditioning in a new rehabilitation program designed by the ultimate denizen of progressive social science, Dr. Brodsky. This reconditioning program, called the "Ludovico process," consists of subjecting Alex to various films of violence, terror, horror, and atrocity; injecting him with a drug to produce nausea; and, to complete the undermining of his psychic apparatus—and, of course, to erase the final vestiges of individuality—accompanying the films and the drug with the music of his beloved Beethoven. Alex watches the violence on the silver screen, retching and vomiting as he does so. The conditioning is pronounced a success, and a meek and pacified Alex reenters society, whereupon he gets a sound thrashing at the library in the same style that he used to administer thrashings himself, before the Ludovico process changed him.

Alex now finds himself in the company of the author F. Alexander, who has written a book called *A Clockwork Orange*. F. Alexander, however, is also the widower of a woman whom Alex and the other droogs had raped and murdered some time before. F. Alexander is unaware of this and proceeds to put Alex into contact with the opposition political party. Since Alex is now a rather well-known personage, as a result of being one of the early successes of the Ludovico process, he is to be exploited. The opposition party parades him about as an example of the deadliness of the ruling party's theory of forcing goodness upon people. To gain full political advantage, the party operatives program Alex to commit suicide, assuming that when he does so the scandal will redound to their electoral benefit. Alex, however, revolts and escapes. He returns to passionate enjoyment of the strains of Beethoven's *Ninth* and to the expression of a semblance of selfhood through that enjoyment.

A Clockwork Orange portrays a future that may seem none too distant to many readers. The droogs are reminiscent of the "Teddy boys" of the 1950s and 1960s and of the "skinhead" youth gangs of the 1970s. While urban violence, especially homicide, remains in Western Europe considerably less prevalent than it is in the United States, the general increase of both psychological and physical violence in recent years is undebatable. The real dilemma in the novel, however, is a moral one. The portrayal is reactionary in its consciousness because it questions precisely the notion of using psychological technology to undermine behavior that is violent and murderous, but that is rooted in individuality. As the prison chaplain explains to Alex, the problem is neither simple nor, of course, is it strictly secular:

> "It may not be nice to be good, little 6655321. It may be horrible to be good. And when I say that to you I realise how self-contradictory that sounds. I know that I shall have many sleepless nights about this. What does God want? Does God want goodness or the choice of goodness? Is a man who chooses the bad perhaps in some way better than the man who has the good imposed upon him?"

For essentially this is the issue. Can there be moral questions in the completely secularized, dehumanized, and sterile world of the progressives? Isn't the freedom of moral choice itself what is deserving of preservation rather than the mere functional reality of good behavior? The reactionary consciousness acknowledges that man may be evil as well as good, that instinct and choice may determine attitude. Not all of experience is simply reducible to the explanation that environment conditions behavior. Good and evil are not reducible to modes of behavior produced by successful conditioning. Humanity is, after all, of fragile and imperfect nature. The technologies that subvert consciousness (the electronic media of *1984*)and that subvert one's psychic being (the psychological programming techniques of *A Clockwork Orange*) are but the first wave of a challenge to human nature by a science and technology serving the cult of secularism and human progress. The progressives, who style themselves fashionably as the ultimate "moderns," comprehend experience only with a grudging literal-mindedness. They fathom neither the transcendent nor the spiritual. "Soul" becomes a word used in Western languages only by priests, poets, and a few popular musicians. Psychology, which claims an inside track on human insight, abandons its literal meaning (from the Greek "psyche" and "logos") of "discourse with the soul" in favor of behaviorism in service to the liberal-progressive myth.

The aspect of reactionary consciousness with which the religious quality of understanding is associated is not, strictly speaking, a political one, though it is often so misconceived. Such was the force of Marx's claim that religion was the "opiate of the masses," a phrase that was so neatly turned around by the historian Raymond Aron shortly after the Second World War, when he proclaimed communism to be the "opiate of the intellectuals." In their temporal conduct, the churches have often proven to be wanting. To confuse this institutional failure with the nature of religion, however, seems a nasty piece of materialist dirty work.

In Western Europe since the Second World War formal religion has waned, especially in the Protestant regions of northern Europe. Religion has changed as well, both with Vatican II, which for all practical purposes closed the centuries-old fissure in Christendom, and with the dialogue—and sporadic indices of accommodation—between the church and the political Left. The Christian tradition was, of course, self-consciously harnessed to a conservative hope right after the Second World War. Wishing to preserve conservative prerogatives while distancing themselves from the discredited reactionary Right, Christian Democratic Parties were founded in postwar Germany and Italy, and the M.R.P. was established under de Gaulle's leadership in France. Yet the trends since 1945 have, in general, supported the growing recognition that religiosity is not necessarily partisan. Nowhere might this be better exemplified than in France. There, right after the Second World War, cadres of "worker priests" declared themselves in solidarity with and in service to the proletariat, a not inconsiderable realignment for a clergy that was still easily associated with antirepublicanism and royalist sentiments a decade or two earlier.

It is not easy, in sum, to estimate just where religiosity and theodicy are integrated into consciousness in the Western world. The secularization of society, and measurable decline of church and clerical strength, represent the waning of the politicized institutional body that made religion manifest on earth. Yet what was made manifest in the buildings and finances, clerical influence, and worldly power was, in the telling words of Charles Péguy, who wrote at the start of the century, religion's *politique*. The deterioration of Christianity into a brittle institutionalization over centuries is a matter of the politicized organs of the church devouring the *mystique* of religiosity itself. But expectations of the institution and its clergy remain surprisingly high even in a secularized world. Rolf Hochuth's ambitious drama *The Deputy* (1961) constitutes an indictment of the Papacy's faint-heartedness and political pragmatism in the face of the Final Solution during the Second World War. The Pope's unwillingness to act forcefully in protest against the murder of Jews is morally condemned. In that condemnation, however, and in the response to the work in many quarters unsympathetic and hostile to the Catholic church, lies a paradox. It may be interpreted that even the secular world expects of it both behavior and action that does not coincide with the view that the church is just another self-interested institution in the modern world. Deep down, even the most dogged critics of the church expect something different, perhaps, in its moral posture. Even after the Holocaust and after the atomic age is upon us, an extraordinary residual claim upon faith, hope, and spirit remains in the Western world.

The perseverance of these values is truly striking. Given the tragedies of the recent past and threats of annihilation in the present, one might have expected them to disappear altogether by now. The decade of the 1950s witnessed, however, even a brief flourish of formal religious conversion, to Roman Catholicism especially, as well as the more bohemian preferences for varieties of mysticism or Eastern religions such as Zen Buddhism. In some measure a certain spirituality influenced at least significant numbers of the New Left. They served as sources of scorn and derision both for materialistic Old Left and Liberal critics, as well as for those whose religiosity remains conventionalized and whose politics are moderate or conservative. The religious point of view has intertwined extensively with the single most pervasive perspective on the human condition in postwar Europe, namely, existentialism. The Catholic reactionary writer Georges Bernanos can be seen as a forerunner. His novels of individual anxiety and guilt framed in fear of loss of God's love date from the 1920s and 1930s. The works of Paul Tillich (a Protestant), Gabriel Marcel (a Roman Catholic), and Martin Buber (a Jew) stand at the front line of those philosophic writings which may be labeled correctly as being both existentialist and religious.

The issue of religiosity is not nearly so simple as it seems. The view that "God is dead" in Nietzschean psychology gave way to a surprisingly benign appraisal of religion as a human projection in Sigmund Freud's commentaries. In the writings of Freud's renegade disciple, Carl Gustav Jung, the religious component in the collective psyche became dominant, as expressed through universal archetypes that point in all instances toward a sense of the transcendant. This religiosity may take different forms.

One form is the theological notion called Manichaeism, which holds that what is wrong with the world is that a true God has been displaced by His evil alter ego. Such a notion lies behind the perception of an older writer, like Bernanos, whose works enact reactionary consciousness. More significantly, it is manifest in a number of the anti-Utopian works, such as those by Anthony Burgess. The other, which is more common because it is less formalized, is the sensibility that recognizes that the pursuit of goodness and equality is limited. Only in a world beyond ours are they achieved. The Swiss dramatist Friedrich Dürrenmatt and the German novelist Günter Grass belong to this category.

In 1967 the Italian Pier Paolo Pasolini made a movie entitlèd *The Gospel According to Saint Matthew*. It is a film composed in neorealistic style. The actors in it are Sicilian peasants, not professionals. The film was shot in black and white on location in the primitive hill villages of Sicily. The settings are barren, and the action is sparse. As a motion picture the production is the antithesis of the great biblical epics of Hollywood, a genre that began in 1924 with Cecil B. DeMille's *The Ten Commandments*.

The Christ of Pasolini's *Gospel* is gentle and humble. His perplexity about his individuality and his very being is authentic. He is a Christ in good faith, whose most fervent message is on behalf of justice for the poor and the oppressed. This is a Christ whose voice thunders but once, when he proclaims that it shall be easier for a camel to go through the eye of a needle than for a rich man to enter the gates of heaven. For this is a Christ in whom the manifestations of individual consciousness and of revolutionary consciousness are combined. He is a Christ, however, who beckons still to a belief in miracles and a faith in God, even if He does not make His hand in the world immanent.

The Gospel According to Saint Matthew is a work that enacts the connectedness of the transcendant with the world of human experience. It does so in ways linking the major modes of consciousness—

the individual, the revolutionary, and the reactionary—which provide in the Western world a mediation of those circumstances that are experienced as life in modern and contemporary times. It suggests, indeed, that these modes are less exclusive and contradictory than they are often assumed to be.

Reactionary consciousness is complex, because the human quest toward demodernization is paradoxical. One paradox has already been alluded to as extreme; for example, reactionary consciousness has long favored a modern institution, the nation state, as a repository for its discharged energy. In another direction, the paradox is manifest in the opposition of the New Left to the very essence of modernization—technocracy and bureaucracy. If this opposition is linked anywhere to the Western revolutionary tradition of the Left, it is all the way back in the earliest "Utopian and humanistic" writings of Karl Marx, prior to 1848, when he began calling his own thinking "scientific." The Old Left's insistence on collectivization, discipline, regimen, and industrial productivity enforced at any human price pales against the humanistic romanticism of the New Left. By the beginning of the 1980s, however, that humanistic romanticism was undergoing transformation. That shift could best be seen in the emerging political and social alliance of ecologists, pacifists, neutralists, feminists, and critics of capitalism. Seeking to organize these disparate concerns into a viable alternative, they did so under the banner of the "Greens," founded in West Germany and soon copied in France ("les Verts").

Epilogue

TO WRITE ABOUT MODERN and contemporary culture in relationship to consciousness is appropriate. "Consciousness," a term that came into use in the early nineteenth century at the dawn of the modern era itself, describes human perception and understanding. This description goes beyond the parameters designated by terms such as "mind," "reason," "thought," and "knowledge." The word "consciousness" provides reference to the emotional (or affective) component that necessarily complements the intellectual (or mental) aspect of awareness, perception, and understanding.

Here I have argued that three of the major modes of consciousness that have persisted in Western culture since the late nineteenth century can be labeled as individual, revolutionary, and reactionary. Although each of these modes of consciousness differs from the other, the sources of inspiration for them are common. Each arises from the attempt to mediate aspects of experience that may be characterized as distinctively modern.

That distinctiveness of modern experience is, in itself problematic. Among the least well understood aspects of modern experience are its variety, discontinuity, and plurality.

The proliferation of forms that edify or gratify different segments of society is one instance of the complexity of contemporary culture. One aspect of the modern experience in society is also confusing; it may be called the "chameleon effect". As we know, many individuals shift radically from politics on the far Left (communism, for example) to the extreme Right (nazism), and vice versa. Religious fanatics are often born out of the disillusionment of rampant amoral hedonism. Abusers of alcohol and other drugs may become righteous devotees of organic foods and apostles of vegetarianism. To most observers, perhaps, such radical shifts in taste, political preference, or values seem to reflect an aberrant personality trait in the individual who undergoes them. Such a view has been popularized, in the United States at least, by Eric Hoffer, whose book the *True Believer* (1951) details a social psychology by which extremism of any sort (or even intense commitment or conviction) is regarded as pathological. In contrast to this view it should be pointed out that the radical embrace of a mode of consciousness in a form close to being pure is not necessarily a sign of mental illness. Moreover, the tendency to abrupt shifts in allegiance and taste may be a characteristic of contemporary culture, with which we may be uneasy because it seems unprecedented in light of what we know of past culture epochs. Nonetheless, rather than being a sign of aberration or pathology, the ability to move easily and quickly from one posture or one taste to another may, in fact, reflect a salutary level of adaptability to contemporary circumstances.

The modes of consciousness here called individual, revolutionary, and reactionary mark the extremes of awareness. Usually, the manifestations of any such mode of consciousness is not direct and pure, in either a cultural work or in an action. A mode of consciousness defines a state of awareness; it is the precondition, or the foundation, of a particular work or action. This caveat certainly does not mean that a mode of consciousness, or a work of art that enacts it, is therefore of secondary importance. Quite the contrary: that which can come to be in experience is based upon the aspect of awareness out of which it comes and in the light of which it is justifiable and comprehensible.

Consciousness relates to action only indirectly and tentatively. The understanding of the interrelationships among culture, thought, society, and politics can never be positivistic or deterministic. To believe that it can be so is one of the major pitfalls of contemporary thought. Actions may, on some occasions, appear to be direct manifestations of a state of consciousness. When this is the case, as with the manifestation of reactionary consciousness on the part of Hitler and the Nazis, an aberration exists. Such manifestation requires a particular collective psychological state that is best described as trancelike. Oddly, then, the direct manifestation of a mode of consciousness requires a certain suspension of the critical faculties—the very faculties normally associated with perception and awareness.

The collective experience that is labeled "history" takes place within the parameters established by the modes of consciousness that exist at particular times. The period since 1870 is distinguished by the plurality of such modes. If ever the descriptive language of movements and epochs and ages applied to human experience, it is only prior to 1870. Since then conflicting modes of consciousness, pluralistic forms, and a variety of taste cultures coexist. George Orwell's fears of a monolithic, present day culture were incorrect. The monolithic domination of human sensibility and perception is more a phenomenon of the Western past than of the present and the near future. During the Middle Ages there was such a domination of culture, namely by the Catholic church. The stirrings of the cultural breakaway from that very domination mark for many the wellspring of modern Western civilization, to which is given the name "Renaissance."

By the last quarter of the twentieth century new technologies afford greater plurality and variety in culture than ever before. They are the conditions of the democratization of cultural enactments and processes. The party bureaucrats in the Soviet Union must keep photocopying machines under lock and key. Rather than being a source of their control of society, the equipment is a challenge to it. What most Orwellians likely fear is not that monolithic control over culture and society may occur. Instead, they fear that the residue of control and domination exercised by self-styled cultural elites of the intelligentsia, taste-makers, academics, and cultural critics will crumble. Throughout the modern and contemporary era the perennial real fear has been not the threat of control, but rather the loss of it. Interestingly, this is perhaps more pronounced in the United States than in Western Europe. In Western European societies social integration is more thorough. The contempt and antagonism between self-styled cultural and intellectual elites and the philistines upon whom they look down is surely more widespread and pernicious in the United States. The stance of cultural and intellectual superiority is a cloak worn by those who accept only grudgingly the democratization that surrounds them.

By the end of the twentieth century all books will not be in musuems, as Marshall McLuhan once peevishly predicted. Even if they were, it would hardly mean that their cultural function in society could not be replicated by other forms and by new technologies. The nostalgia for the end product of moveable-type print as it appears on the page is gratuitous, and is becoming, in any case, quickly outmoded.

It is at this juncture that I should underscore what has become obvious throughout this book. In the Western world, during the first three-quarters of the twentieth century, the feature-length fiction movie has gradually and successfully supplanted the novel. This rise and triumph of the motion picture has displaced literature proper from being the centerpiece of our widely shared mimetic culture. Although the novel has by no means disappeared, the literary impulse has been redirected extensively into new and experimental forms, with a number of authors in France taking the lead in this effort. Moreover, the motion picture has shown signs of becoming a form with a variety of new possibilities.

The philosophical and ideological roles of novels, plays, and movies have increased exponentially in the twentieth century. In part this is so because of the relative eclipse of academic, or formal, philosophy. In the late nineteenth century Friedrich Nietzsche pointed toward this development with his debunking of past system-building and his astute commentaries on the arbitrary, irrational, subconscious, and highly personal sources of what the Western world had come to venerate as high-minded and aloof examination of problems. The processes of social change and the increased democratization of Western societies (even given the setbacks of the 1920s and 1930s) have also contributed to this situation. The novel, the play, and the movie are all forms that require high levels of concentration and intense participation by the reader or viewer. Each also has become standardized in modes that allow for extensive development of the basic elements of representationalism, such as character portrayal, setting, theme, and so forth. Other forms that are popular in the contemporary world, such as popular songs, are not commonly developed in length and scope adequate for them to challenge novels, plays, or movies on their own plane. Nor, for that matter, are the technologies that proffer a combination of narrative entertainment, dramatic content, information, and opinion—namely, radio and television—competitive in this regard. For radio and television are technologies rather than forms of expression. Moreover, both radio and television are used randomly just as much as (or more than) they are used in a state of concentrated awareness. Because of their nature, then, and the ways in which they are used, neither radio nor television manifests consciousness directly, as do novels, plays, and movies.

Another line of commentary that has been suggested in this essay is that the epoch of Romanticism, which can be dated roughly 1780–1850, is the watershed for the modes of consciousness discussed here. Individual, revolutionary, and reactionary consciousness may be understood as paralleling the established romantic passions for interiority and personal experience, for a radical breaking down of restraint and injustice, and for a kind of spiritualistic nostalgia for the distant past. These interests and intentions were not easily accommodated to one another. And it might be said that the romantic mode—full of contradictions, inconsistencies, and paradoxes—marks the very attitudes and perceptions within which modern and contemporary consciousness has emerged. It is in the attempt either to force to unchallenged supremacy one of these primary modes of consciousness, or to mediate between them by overcoming the dissonances, that much of contemporary awareness exists. The struggle of what came to be called the New Left in Western societies by the late 1960s seemed aimed, after all, at just such mediation. The contradictory combination of elements that characterized the New Left—sexual freedom and social conscience, nostalgia for a return to nature and progressive notions of society, hedonistic personal gratification and demands for economic equality—constituted an almost random array of attitudes and desires traceable to the Romantic era proper.

Romanticism, it might be said, was not so much a movement in the various areas of artistic creativity, as it was a prolonged shift in consciousness that posited a fundamental pattern of ambivalent, contradictory, and often paradoxical responses to life and society. That pattern perished with the coming of an era after 1848 characterized by confidence, materialism, optimism, and science. It began reemerging shortly before the First World War, advanced randomly and often crazily between the two wars, and then came forth once the dust had settled after World War II.

Yet, throughout we are talking about consciousness. And so talking is not to be confused with the discussion of themes or ideas, although both are a part of and also attributable to modes of consciousness. For this reason, while a fair degree of attention is given here to Western Europe since 1945, major themes in its culture have not been mentioned. In passing, those would certainly include the attempts to come to terms with the experiences of dictatorship and the Second World War. As an extension of that general theme, the exploration of the nature of collective guilt, treated frequently in a style that reaches back all the way to Ancient Greece, would be reckoned too as an abiding concern. Yet a third theme, which is also a direct consequence of the Second World War and its aftermath, is the mediation of aspects of Western European relationships with the United States. The issue of those relationships goes well beyond economic, political, and military ties, and has much to do with

Western European self-image, a collective sense of independence and integrity and of the value of that perspective on experience that remains essentially European.

Throughout this book I have tried to point out the fact that Western Europe remains the center of that civilization that we call Western. This is an extremely important matter. For as Western Europeans regain the temporarily lost sense of their integrity and of the centrality of their culture to the contemporary world, a number of consequences will follow.

The ten nations which by the 1980s composed the official Western European community have a population of roughly 250 million. Whether they have definitively overcome what I have called the "European disease" of nationalism remains to be seen. The signs that they have done so are encouraging. It would be highly unlikely, if not unthinkable, for the German Federal Republic to declare war on France in the 1980s, or for some belligerency to occur that might actively engage England and Italy on opposite sides. All sorts of differences abound in the experience of the Western European peoples. Whether these amount to anything more serious than the regionalism found anywhere that is georgraphically large and quite populous—say, the United States, the Soviet Union, or China—is arguable.

In their own ways, both the United States and the Soviet Union were, at Western Europe's "hour zero" in 1945, the heirs to the Western tradition, or at least to substantial portions of it. They were the two likely powers to lead humanity in the quest for accommodation with the complexity of modern life. Subsequently, although for very different reasons, both have squandered these opportunities. Both societies demonstrate enormously rich examples of their virtuosity and their resoluteness in many ways. Among those demonstrations, however, is little that grasps the complexity of advancing those modes of consciousness through which future experience will be dealt with and made meaningful. Western Europe holds far more promise than either of the superpowers in that regard.

It would be a stunning paradox were Western Europe to become the conscience of the world between 1980 and the dawn of the twenty-first century. Between 1870 and 1914 Europe claimed world dominance, a dominance based on the presumed ascendancy of rationalism, science, and technology overwritten by a high-handed racism and underwritten by commercial successes. Europe squandered its claim through self-inflicted violence beginning in 1914 and in the rise of right-wing authoritarianism that led from the First World War to the Second. Yet from the psychic exhaustion, material destruction, and moral bankruptcy of 1945 a newly pacified, humbled, and more deeply sensitive Western Europe has emerged. Metaphors of Western Europe's "rebirth" or "Renaissance" since 1945 are, however, fanciful. It is more apt to speak of Western European sensibility as making progress beyond naiveté toward maturity.

Learning to live with modernization is no easy job. As we know all too well, with Hitler and Stalin pointing out the extremes, it can often be a deadly business. There is no real way around modernization, nor can its extension nearly everywhere be halted indefinitely. One challenge for the future is the amelioration and mediation of the three modes of consciousness discussed here. They do not encompass every aspect of modern experience. They do, however, point to the fundamental categories of collective psychology that are most important in coming to terms with the tensions and anxieties of contemporary life.

Annotated Bibliography

THE NOVELS AND PLAYS referred to throughout the book are generally available in English translations, if not originally published in English. Most of the movies mentioned can be found, either with English subtitles or dubbed into English voice, in theatrical or 16mm distribution. Listing of these primary sources, on which the book is based, is not made here.

These annotated references are to secondary works, which are, in varying degrees, germane to the topics of the book. Works on which the author has drawn heavily are marked with an asterisk (*).

*Armstrong, Robert Plant. *The Affecting Presence*. Urbana: University of Illinois Press, 1971.

This essay by anthropologist/aesthetician Armstrong considers what we call the "work of art" in the Western world as simply a special instance of "affecting presence." A bold and sweeping attempt to create a new human aesthetic.

*Armstrong, Robert Plant. *Wellspring*. Berkeley: University of California Press, 1976.

An extension of Armstrong's earlier writing in *The Affecting Presence*. This essay explores the collective dynamic of the relationship of the work of affecting presence to culture. In particular, the comments on twentieth-century Euro-American culture, while brief, are extraordinarily lucid.

Arnold, Matthew. *Culture and Anarchy*. Cambridge: The University Press, 1932.

A classic defense of "high" culture against the charge that it is not relevant to the real problems of life. Arnold argues the standardized view that culture has an important function in the quest toward the perfection of humanity. Originally published 1844.

Becker, Howard Paul. *Man in Reciprocity: Introductory Lectures on Culture, Society, and Personality*. New York: Praeger, 1956.

Lectures designed for introduction to anthropology and sociology. Culture viewed in a relatively personalized explanation of its functions.

*Benda, Julien. *The Betrayal of the Intellectuals*. New York: William Morrow Co., 1928 (tr. Richard Aldington).

An original and searing indictment of the sell-out by European intellectuals to the passion of nationalism after 1870. Benda pleads for restoration of the true calling of the *clerc* which is disinterested in partisanship and nobly high-minded.

*Berger, Peter, Brigitte Berger, and Hansfried Kellner. *The Homeless Mind: Modernization and Consciousness*. New York: Random House, 1973.

A very compelling essay, rooted in a Weberian thesis. The Bergers and Kellner analyze the psychology of man's attempts to deal with the two fundamental elements of modernization—technology and bureaucratization. Compared to most sociological writing, this is relatively free of jargon.

Berger, Peter, and Thomas Luckman. *The Social Construction of Reality*. Garden City, N.Y.: Doubleday, 1967.

A systematic and generalized account of the role of knowledge in society. In examining society as both an objective and as a subjective phenomenon, the authors argue that sociological investigation must be carried out as a humanistic discipline.

Bettelheim, Bruno. *The Informed Heart: Autonomy in a Mass Age*. New York: Avon Books, 1971.

Bettelheim examines the problems of achieving self-realization and preserving freedom in a mass society. He argues poignantly against the increasing pressures toward dehumanization.

*Binion, Rudolph. *Hitler Among the Germans*. New York/Oxford/Amsterdam: Elsevier, 1976.

A virtuoso exploration of the personal psychological roots of Hitler's obsessions and how these intermeshed with the collective psychological needs of the German people. Accounting for the personal sources of Hitler's anti-Semitism in light of the collective context is here especially compelling.

*Binion, Rudolph. *Soundings: Psychohistorical and Psycholiterary*. New York: Psychohistory Press, 1981.

A collection of essays written over two decades. Of special interest for students of culture and society are the pieces on Kafka's *Metamorphosis* and on Pirandello. The essay entitled "Hitler Looks East" gives a succinct and compelling view of how anti-Semitism took hold in Hitler's thought right after the First World War.

*Bistray, Georges. *Marxist Models of Literary Realism*. New York: Columbia University Press, 1978.

This surprisingly readable study treats varying attitudes toward literature and what it should be on the political Left. Very useful for clarifying the different perspectives from which Marxists may view mimetic art and society; a well-balanced treatment.

Burns, Elizabeth, and Tom Burns (eds.). *Sociology of Literature and Drama*. Middlesex: Penguin Press, 1973.

A volume of essays examining various perspectives on literature and drama in society. This is a well-balanced volume that presents many perspectives (ideologies) and draws on examples from numerous epochs.

Camus, Albert. *The Rebel*. New York: Vintage Books, 1956 (tr. Anthony Bower).

Essays examining the idea of rebellion. Camus develops an incisive (and some would say reactionary) view of human solidarity based on man's rebellion against the conditions of life itself.

Caudwell, Christopher. *Studies and Further Studies in a Dying Culture*. New York/London: Monthly Review Press, 1971.

A collection of essays from the 1930s in which the author heaps damnation upon bourgeois culture and all the decadence of its forms. A view from the Left that is an orthodox indictment of Western culture, but which is blessed with witty prose and clear argumentation.

Caute, David. *The Left in Europe Since 1789*. New York: McGraw-Hill, 1966.

A history and description of leftist thought and political movements in Europe.

Eliot, Thomas Sterns. *Notes Towards the Definition of Culture*. New York: Harcourt, Brace, 1949.

An attempt to define the word "culture." Eliot argues that culture is essentially related to religion. In particular, he polemicizes against the lowering of educational standards in the name of democratization and the tendency of politics to dominate culture.

Ellul, Jacques. *The Betrayal of the West*. New York: Seabury, 1978 (tr. M. J. O'Connell).

A defense of reason, self-awareness, self-criticism, freedom, and individualism. Ellul fears that technology compromises and threatens to eliminate the lot of them.

Ellul, Jacques. *The Technological Society*. New York: A. Knopf, 1964 (tr. John Wilkinson).

Ellul examines the effects on modern man of the rationalization of life manifested in the idea of "technique." He shows the penetration of "technique" into every aspect of human experience.

Enzensberger, Hans-Magnus. *The Consciousness Industry*. New York: Seabury, 1974 (tr. Michael Roloff).

A perceptive "new-lefist" critique of contemporary culture and attitudes about it. Enzensberger argues on behalf of democratization in literature, politics, and the media. A cautious, yet surprisingly optimistic appraisal of Western man's prospects; compare this with Caudwell's death song for the bourgeoisie.

Feuer, Lewis. *Marx and the Intellectuals*. New York: Anchor Books, 1969.

Essays on the response of intellectuals to Marxism. Feuer examines why the alienated intellectuals have so often made Marxism their hobby-horse.

Fischer, Ernst. *The Necessity of Art*. London: Penguin Books, 1963 (tr. Anna Bostock).

An ambitious and highly logical explanation of the generalized Marxist view of art. Fischer's is really the first of the revisions that permit a Marxist explanation of most of modern art.

Freud, Sigmund. *Civilization and its Discontents*. New York: Norton & Co., 1962 (tr. James Strachey).

First published in 1929, Freud's essay on the conflict between individual demands for freedom and civilization's limits is bleak and problematic. Civilization, it turns out, is possible only at the price of a certain measure of individual self-renunciation. Instinct is aggressive, and civilization is a tenuous affair that may be making us mentally ill.

Friedell, Egon. *A Cultural History of the Modern Age: The Crisis of the European Soul from the Black Death to the World War.* New York: Knopf, 1930. 3 vols. (tr. Charles Atkinson).

A forerunner in the viewing of culture holistically. A wise, witty, and very perceptive multi-volume work.

*Fromm, Erich. *Escape from Freedom.* New York: Avon Books, 1965.

From a social-psychological perspective Fromm examines the burden that freedom places on the individual. In particular, he sees problems in the theological freedom of Protestantism and the economic freedom of *laissez-faire* capitalism. He writes compellingly on the appeal of totalitarianism to the alienated and the unloved. A pioneer study, first published in 1941.

Fromm, Erich. *To Have or To Be?* New York: Harper & Row, 1976.

An analysis of the collective dimensions of selfishness and altruism viewed as basic character traits. He relates the crisis of this antagonism to contemporary life, calling for a new synthesis that he labels "The City of Being."

*Gans, Herbert. *Popular Culture and High Culture.* New York: Basic Books, 1974.

A lucid and discerning essay on the problem of culture in the modern age. Gans advances a theory of differing taste cultures that describes contemporary cultural pluralism and diversity.

Glicksberg, Charles. *The Literature of Commitment.* Lewisburg, Pa.: Bucknell University Press, 1976.

A study of various modes of "engaged" literary activity in the twentieth century. Lucid, but highly selective. Nonetheless, Glicksberg gives nearly equal attention to right-wing literati and to those of the Left—admirably.

*Hayes, Carlton J. H. *A Generation of Materialism, 1871–1900.* New York and London: Harper Bros., 1941.

A standard, if dated, treatment of the last three decades of the nineteenth century in Europe. The changes which constituted the so-called second industrial revolution are described well. A later book by the same author, *Contemporary Europe Since 1870* [publ. 1958], recounts some similar materials.

Hughes, H. Stuart. *Consciousness and Society: The Reorientation of European Social Thought, 1890–1930.* New York: Vintage Books, 1958.

An intellectual history of the social thought that has shaped the twentieth-century mind and sensibility. Hughes examines deftly the impact and interaction of various social theories on modern consciousness.

Izenberg, Gerald. *The Existentialist Critique of Freud.* Princeton: Princeton University Press, 1977.

A detailed portrayal of the critique of Freud in post-1945 Continental European thought. Izenberg provides valuable insights, both into psycho-analysis and existentialism. The differences in regard to the individual are emphasized.

Jarvie, Ian C. *Movies as Social Criticism.* Metuchen: Scarecrow Press, 1978.

A perceptive volume that explores the potential social value of movies. Although almost all of Jarvie's examples are Hollywood films, the interpretive implications go well beyond the U.S. Might be read in conjunction with the same author's *Movies and Society* (1971).

Johnson, Lesley. *The Cultural Critics: From Matthew Arnold to Raymond Williams.* Boston: Routledge & Kegan Paul, 1979.

A study of the concept of culture as employed by British thinkers and commentators since mid-nineteenth century. An attempt to elucidate the moral visions and social critiques associated with differing views of culture.

Johnson, R. A. *The Long March of the French Left.* New York: St. Martin's, 1981.

An examination of the French Left, emphasizing its advances and defeats after 1968. Extensive treatment of the changing social structure and political sociology of contemporary France is presented.

Jowett, Garth, and James M. Linton. *Movies as Mass Communication.* Beverly Hills: Sage, 1980.

A valuable general study on the movies, with ample material on the medium's psychological, sociological, political, and cultural role in twentieth-century societies.

Kahler, Erich. *The Tower and the Abyss.* New York: Viking, 1969.

An examination of the effects of collectivization on modern man as reflected in cultural and intellectual life. Kahler here first presents his arguments on behalf of our achieving a new human community.

Kirk, Russell. *The Conservative Mind from Burke to Santayana*. Chicago: Henry Regnery Co., 1953.

A history and critique of conservative political thought.

Lasch, Christopher. *The Culture of Narcissism: American Life in an Age of Dimishing Expectations*. New York: Warner Books, 1979.

An analysis of life in the U.S. in terms of the self-centered personality dominant in the 1970s. Lasch finds this personality type contributing to the trivialization of modern life and culture. Speculative, but interesting to compare to what may be discerned in Western Europe.

Laurenson, Diana, and Alan Swingewood. *The Sociology of Literature*. New York: Schocken Books, 1972.

An interesting attempt at tracing the bases of a sociology of literature. Jointly written, it is uneven in spots. The first section, Swingewood's, on a theory of literature and society, is a neat overview of a complex topic.

Lukacs, Georg. *Marxism and Human Liberation*. New York: Dell, 1973 (tr. & ed. E. San Juan, Jr.).

These essays by the Marxist philosopher and literary critic are so compelling as to cause even a reader who is suspicious of Marxism to take notice of them. The collection spans the philosophical, aesthetic, and political observations of one of the Left's most perceptive commentators on culture.

*Lukacs, John. *The Passing of the Modern Age*. New York: Harper & Row, 1970.

A conservative's view of the decline of Western civilization. His perspective ranges from comments on the degeneration of the arts into "senselessness and primitivism" to our consciousness of the past and the decaying of the scientific myth. Carefully argued and compelling.

Marcuse, Herbert. *Eros and Civilization*. Boston: Beacon Press, 1966.

Marcuse applied revisionist Freudianism to social theory, calling for a less repressive civilization. In its day a handbook sometimes of the New Left, this is a delightful polemic on behalf of human freedom and the goodness of human nature.

*McLuhan, Marshall. *Understanding Media*. New York: Bantam Books, 1966.

As much a victim of his success and popularity as perhaps any cultural critic has been, McLuhan here explores the relationship of the media, culture, consciousness, and what he called the shrinking global village.

In spite of his many historical gaffes and bizarre claims, his writing is extraordinarily important.

Monaco, James. *The New Wave*. New York: Oxford University Press, 1976.

One of the rare books that treats cinema perceptively with regard to a particular epoch of European movie-making. In this instance a prolific writer's work is on mark, especially with its treatment of the films of Jean-Luc Godard.

Monaco, Paul. *Cinema and Society: France and Germany during the Twenties*. New York/Oxford/Amsterdam: Elsevier, 1976.

A treatment of national cinema in France and Germany during the 1920s. Analyses approximately one hundred popular films in terms of the collective psychological import of their contents.

Mosse, George L. (ed.), *Literature and Politics in the Twentieth Century*. New York: Harper and Row, 1967.

A volume that treats literature and literary figures in relationship to society. Any number of perspectives and approaches are represented in the numerous selections. F. Bondy writing on Sartre, D. Jacobson's article on D.H. Lawrence, and J. Raskin's comments on Conrad's *Heart of Darkness* may be of greatest interest for readers of *Modern European Culture and Consciousness*.

Mosse, George L., *Masses and Man: Nationalist and Fascist Perceptions of Reality*. New York: H. Fertig, 1980.

An attempt to analyze and describe the common elements in ultra-right wing ideologies. A great deal of attention is given, in particular, to Nazi Germany. Mosse reveals a willingness to take into account the elements and forms of "popular culture."

Mumford, Lewis. *The Myth of the Machine: Technics and Human Development*. New York: Harcourt, Brace, Jovanovich, 1967.

A reexamination of the notion of man as the "tool-using animal." Mumford argues for an understanding of technics that is "life-centered" rather than "work-centered."

Nisbet, Robert. *The Quest for Community*. London: Oxford University Press, 1969.

Nisbet argues that the centralization of power in modern society has led to loss of a traditional sense of community. His preference is for a political order that is decentralized and pluralistic.

Nolte, Ernst. *Three Faces of Fascism: Action Française, Italian Fascism, National Socialism.* New York: New American Library, 1969 (tr. Leila Vennewitz).

Nolte equates three right-wing movements, arguing that all three were reflections of the same common quest. An able, if problematic, attempt at structural analysis of the right-wing terror that swept Europe after the First World War.

Ortega y Gasset, José. *The Revolt of the Masses.* New York: Norton, 1957.

Ortega's classic examination of modern culture in light of the threats posed to humanity by the rise of mass society. Originally published in 1930.

Revel, Jean-Francois. *The Totalitarian Temptation.* New York: Doubleday, 1977 (tr. David Hapgood).

The world is evolving toward a socialist order, Revel argues. In that evolution he sees the main obstacle not as capitalism but rather as communism.

*Rieff, Philip. *The Triumph of the Therapeutic.* New York: Harper & Row, 1966.

An argument in favor of the view that in the twentieth century thought, culture, and consciousness have been swept up in the notion of "psychological man."

Schorske, Carl E., *Fin-de-Siecle Vienna: Politics and Culture.* New York: Knopf, 1980.

Schorske writes on a variety of characteristics of Viennese life and culture prior to the First World War. This volume enjoyed a good audience beyond academic circles when it was first published.

Snow, C. P. *The Two Cultures and the Scientific Revolution.* New York: Cambridge Univeristy Press, 1959.

A polemic addressed to the discontinuity in Western culture. Snow argues that the difficulties in communication and the differences in worldview between scientists and humanists characterize the split. Generally he seems to hold the humanists (or literary types) more responsible for the dilemma.

Sorokin, Pitirim. *The Crisis of Our Age: Essays in Socialism and Philosophy.* New York: E. P. Dutton, 1941.

An analysis of modern culture in transition. The author contends that Western culture is disintegrating and will be replaced by a new form.

*Sorlin, Pierre. *The Film in History: Restaging the Past.* Oxford: Basil & Blackwood, 1980.

A social historian's attempt to examine the way in which movies with historical settings have created a perception of the past. The discussions here of *The Grand Illusion* and *Open City* are especially valuable. Strong theory blends with accurate analysis of the films.

*Steiner, George. *In Bluebeard's Castle: Some Notes toward the Redefinition of Culture.* New Haven: Yale University Press, 1967.

Steiner explores the disintegration of Western culture. He sees the Holocaust as representing the final demise of a culture of exhausted possibilities. He proposes some possible future directions for Western culture.

Stern, Fritz R., *The Politics of Cultural Despair: A Study in the Rise of German Ideology.* Berkeley: University of California Press, 1961.

A treatment of the particular shifts in German intellectual and cultural life at the end of the nineteenth century which, according to the author's thesis, helped pave the way for National Socialism after World War I. Stern deals most extensively with three figures: Langbehn, Lagarde, and Moeller van der Brück.

*Stromberg, Roland N. *After Everything: Western Intellectual History since 1945.* New York: St. Martin's Press, 1975.

A very able attempt at surveying the myriad directions in thought and culture in Western Europe and the United States since the end of the Second World War. Stromberg's assessment of the rise of the New Left is compelling, although his biases against its anti-intellectualism may strain some readers. A surprisingly deft job of synthesis for trying to cover so much in a short space.

Tillich, Paul. *Theology of Culture.* New York: Oxford University Press, 1964 (ed. R. C. Kimball).

Reflections on the religious dimension of cultural activities. Tillich discusses this dimension in relationship to art, existential philosophy, psychoanalysis, science, and education.

Tönnies, Ferdinand. *Community and Society.* East Lansing: Michigan State University Press, 1957 (tr. C. P. Loomis).

The classic formulation of the two different types of society, *Gemeinschaft* and *Gesellschaft*. The former is based on fundamental human relationships, the latter on rational and utilitarian values.

Trilling, Lionel. *Sincerity and Authenticity*. Cambridge: Harvard University Press, 1974.

An examination of the themes of sincerity and authenticity in Western literature and thought. Trilling, in particular, explores the moral implications of the modern idea of authenticity.

Viereck, Peter. *Conservatism: From John Adams to Churchill*. Princeton, N.J.: Van Nostrand, 1956.

A history of political conservative thought. Viereck includes a definition of conservatism and the changing social context to which this thought has responded since the early nineteenth century.

*Vogel, Amos. *Film as a Subversive Art*. New York: Random House, 1974.

A rare, valuable book on the varieties of avant-garde, revolutionary, or political movies. Much of the book is given over to brief descriptions of individual movies, making the text at times more like a catalogue than an essay. Part Four, "Towards A New Consciousness," may be of particular interest.

Weiss, John. *The Fascist Tradition: Radical Right-Wing Extremism in Modern Europe*. New York: Harper & Row, 1967.

Weiss labels fascism as a particular form of right-wing extremism. Careful and discriminating, the study remains an excellent basic consideration of the topic.

*Whyte, Lancelot. *The Unconscious before Freud*. New York: St. Martin's Press, 1978.

An extraordinarily perceptive analysis of the understanding of theories of consciousness and the unconscious prior to the twentieth century. The treatment of nineteenth-century experimental psychology in Continental Europe is especially strong.

*Wilkinson, James. *The Intellectual Resistance in Europe*. Cambridge: Harvard University Press, 1980.

A skillful and highly original treatment of the underground movements in Europe during the years of the Nazi occupation of various territories, 1939–1945. The interpretations of the changes and refinements which occurred and which pointed to new intellectual and cultural directions after the Second World War are compelling.

Williams, Raymond. *Culture and Society, 1780–1950*. New York: Harper & Row, 1966.

Williams examines the evolution of the word "culture" in its English usage. From this he draws implications about the wider changes in society to which the change in usage is related.

Index of Persons

Index of Titles
(Films, Novels, Plays, Essays, etc.)